Twayne's United States Authors Series

Sylvia E. Bowman, *Editor*

INDIANA UNIVERSITY

Ruth Suckow

RUTH SUCKOW

By LEEDICE McANELLY KISSANE

Idaho State University

 142

Twayne Publishers, Inc.   ::   New York

Preface

THE NAME Ruth Suckow was well known in the 1920's, when Realistic treatments of the Middle West were the vogue in American fiction. During the first fifteen years of her writing career, she published some forty short stories and critical essays, three novelettes, and six novels. All her fiction had Iowa settings; all bore the hallmark of convincing authenticity. The young author possessed a truth-telling temperament and a total disdain for pretentiousness. Her literary style, acquired through unremitting self-discipline, reflected these qualities. Quiet and restrained, it was characterized by detachment and almost stark simplicity. Yet her critical comments struck home. The rebels of the Realistic movement claimed her as their own.

In the 1930's, when regional writing was under scrutiny, Miss Suckow's works were often noted as exemplars. As Sinclair Lewis put it, they were "genuinely native." Gifted with a poetic sense of place, the young writer valued the local quality as "that which gives form, color, and flavor"; but she hastened to add that "It does not give ultimate significance." She discovered beauty in commonplace surroundings, worth in ordinary lives, and pathos in undistinguished human struggle. In the Midwestern character, she perceived "a certain downright quality, a plainness, a simple freshness." Her assessment of the "folks" culture, dominated by the common desire to "get ahead," was central in all her early works and culminated in her important novel *The Folks*.

Though Ruth Suckow was justly classified as a Realist and as a regionalist, she was something more. That "something more" has never been adequately assessed. Most of her early critics were satisfied to exclaim over her scrupulous fidelity to her chosen locale and its people; later, as her books and stories appeared less frequently, commentators failed to analyze them in depth. Scholarly appraisals of her works are rare, and are confined for the most part to brief (though laudatory) mentions in general studies of fiction of the period. Aside from one unpublished doctoral dissertation, no full-length study of her work in its entirety has appeared. It is a regrettable fact that at the time of her death in 1960, Ruth Suckow and her works were not as well known as they had been thirty years earlier at the height of her career. Yet her books are not period pieces or local-color oddities. Though they reflect their region and their era, they have universality. They deserve a place in the chronicle of American literary achievement.

Miss Suckow was a lover of order—of putting first things first. She would recognize that to judge an author, one must first know what he has to say. Hence, this brief study undertakes to present, with a certain amount of explication, the writings of Ruth Suckow in the order of their appearance, linked with such circumstances of the author's life as bore an influence on them. More detailed analyses of her literary techniques may appropriately follow this introductory work.

Ruth Suckow devotes its first chapter to an account of the beginnings of its subject's career. The author's search for beauty, as first expressed in lyric poems and evidenced in the early short stories of *Iowa Interiors*, is traced in the next chapter. In Chapter 3, quests for self-fulfillment are illustrated in the novelettes, in *Country People*, and in *Odyssey of a Nice Girl*. Feminism, another of Miss Suckow's salient interests, is explored in the chapter entitled "Women" which includes *The Bonney Family*, *Cora*, *The Kramer Girls*, and the short stories in *Children and Older People*. The next chapter considers Miss Suckow's cultural theory regarding "the folks" in the novel by that name. "Memories" examines the novel *New Hope* and the short stories in *Some Others and Myself*, including the "Memoir" written about the author's father. The last novel, *The John Wood Case*, is the subject of the chapter "Resolution"; and the final chapter includes a summing-up and suggestions as to the place Ruth Suckow may justly be expected to occupy in American literature.

To study the life work of Ruth Suckow is to come to know her as a person—a rare and rewarding privilege. The first books are the blossoming product of her youthful inspiration; the later, more topical ones the fruits of her diligent search for answers to problems of her time and place. The final ones were long in the making and represent the very distillation of her intellectual and spiritual effort. Honesty and regard for the beauty of order and moderation are evident in all she wrote, but her artistry is beyond explaining and can only be enjoyed.

LEEDICE KISSANE

Acknowledgments

I am indebted to the Faculty Research Committee of Idaho State University, Professor Albert E. Taylor, chairman, for financial grants enabling me to carry on this study.

Several individuals gave generously of their advice and assistance, chief among them Mr. Ferner Nuhn, without whose sincere and friendly help I could scarcely have undertaken it. Professor John T. Frederick showed me great kindness in writing helpfully about his acquaintance with Ruth Suckow, as did Professor Clyde C. Tull, Mrs. John M. Bridgham, and Mrs. Aimée Buchanan. Mr. Frank Paluka of the Special Collections Department of the University Libraries, State University of Iowa; Mr. Henry Alden, Librarian, Grinnell College; and Miss Alice McClain, formerly Associate Librarian, Idaho State University, have rendered me services beyond the call of duty. Many other persons, too numerous to list, gave valuable information; their interest attests to the warmth of feeling Miss Suckow inspired in her fellow human beings.

Much gratitude is due Professor Margaret O'Brien Stewart for permitting me to make use of the chronology of events of Ruth Suckow's life prepared for her doctoral dissertation, "A Critical Study of Ruth Suckow's Fiction," to Professor Sylvia E. Bowman for her thoughtful editing of my manuscript; and to Miss Kathleen Isaac, Director of Clerical Services, Idaho State University, for her professional competence in typing it.

I wish to make further acknowledgment to the following: To Random House and Alfred A. Knopf and to John T. Frederick for permission to quote from his essay "A Literary Evening, Iowa Style" in *Borzoi, 1925;* to Abigail Ann Hamblen and the Cornell College *Husk* for permission to quote from her article "The Poetry of Place" in the March, 1961, issue; to Ferner Nuhn and the *Iowan* for permission to quote from the series "The Cycle of Seasons in Iowa" in issues of October-November, 1960; December-January, 1960-61; February-March, 1961; and April-May, 1961.

To Ferner Nuhn for permission to quote from Ruth Suckow's letters now in the Special Collections department of the University of Iowa Libraries and to the following for permission to quote from letters to Miss Suckow: to Blanche Knopf; John Farrar; and to the estates of Sigrid Undset, Dorothy Canfield Fisher, Robert Frost, and Henry L. Mencken.

Contents

Chronology

1892   Ruth Suckow born August 6, Hawarden, Iowa, to William John Suckow, son of John and Caroline Suckow, natives of the dukedom of Mecklenburg, Germany, and Anna Mary Kluckhohn, whose father, Reverend Charles Kluckhohn, a Methodist minister, came from the small city of Lippe-Detmold in the province of Lippe.

1894   Father accepted pastorate of Congregational Church at LeMars, Iowa, town of five thousand, which he held for one year. During this time Ruth and her sister, Emma, lived with an aunt in Paulina, Iowa, while their mother was receiving medical treatment; first in Hawarden; then in Kirksville, Missouri; and later in St. Paul.

1896   Family returned to Hawarden to live.

1898   Father accepted pastorate at Algona, Iowa. There Ruth attended Central School.

1901   In the summer the family went to Buffalo to attend the Pan-American Exposition, to Albany to visit relatives, and to Boston.

1902   In the spring, father accepted a church at Fort Dodge where he stayed for three years. Emma graduated from high school; Ruth attended Wabkonsa School.

1906   The family moved to Manchester, Iowa, the county seat of Delaware County. This pastorate was held for one year.

1907   Father began a three-year field service for Grinnell College. The girls attended school there.

1910   After Ruth's graduation from high school at Grinnell the family moved to Davenport where Reverend Suckow became pastor of the Edwards Congregational Church. Ruth matriculated at Grinnell College; specialized in English. While Ruth was at Grinnell, Emma married Edwin O. Hunting, a Grinnell College classmate. They had two children, Robert Suckow Hunting and Judith Ann Hunting.

1912   Father resigned from the ministry to take a position writting lectures for the Victor Animatograph Company, manufacturer of stereopticons and moving pictures, in Davenport, Iowa. Father purchased forty acres of land, twenty miles west of Mobile, Alabama.

1913　Ruth left Grinnell College in June. While a student at Grinnell, she spent one summer as a waitress in Yellowstone Park.

1914　Emma moved to Colorado for her health.

1915　Ruth graduated from the Curry School of Expression in Boston and came home to be with her father who had returned to the ministry and accepted in January his second pastorate at Manchester, Iowa. Ruth spent a month with her mother and Emma at Colorado Springs. Enrolled in the University of Denver.

1916　Father's church building destroyed by fire on November 24.

1917　Ruth received a Bachelor of Arts from the University of Denver.

1917-　For one year was assistant to Dr. Ida Kruse McFarlane,
1918　Head of the Department of English, University of Denver. Received a Master of Arts in English, University of Denver. After receiving degree, spent one winter as employee of a map company in Denver. Wrote material for automobile guide books.

1918　First published poem, "An Old Woman in a Garden," appeared in *Touchstone* in August. "Song in October," poem, published in *The Midland*, September-October.

1919　In Denver learning apiary business from Miss Delia Weston. Mother died and was brought to Garner, Iowa, for services in the Congregational church and for burial. Father's resignation from Manchester pastorate to be effective in October. He and Ruth made a trip to Mobile, Alabama. Later he accepted a pastorate at Earlville, Iowa. Ruth moved to the parsonage with him and established her "Orchard Apiary" at the edge of town.

1920　Emma lost her son.

1921 First published story, "Uprooted," in *The Midland* for February. Father began pastorate at Forest City, May 1, 1921. "By Hill and Dale," poem, published in *Poetry*, June.

1921- For six months editorial assistant on *The Midland*.
1922

1922 January 25 at Cedar Falls her father married Mrs. Opal Swindle. She had two sons, Earl and Duane Swindle. During the winter of 1922-23 Ruth lived with them.

1923 Emma died of tuberculosis. "A Part of the Institution," a short novel, published in *Smart Set*, October.

1924 *Country People* first published serially in *The Century Magazine*, later by Knopf. From 1924 to 1934 lived in New York in winters; kept bees in Earlville during the summer.

1925 *The Odyssey of a Nice Girl.*

1926 *Iowa Interiors.* Ellan McIlvaine became literary agent. At Miss McIlvaine's death Marie F. Rodell became agent.

1926 *The Bonney Family.* Father accepted his last pastorate at Alden, Iowa.

1929 On March 11 in San Diego California, Ruth married Ferner Nuhn, son of Mr. and Mrs. William C. Nuhn. Cedar Falls, Iowa. Lived in Santa Fe until November, 1929. *Cora.*

1930 *The Kramer Girls.* Honorary degree awarded by Grinnell College to Ruth Suckow.

1931 *Children and Older People.* Lived in McGregor, Iowa, part of the year.

1931- Lived in Cedar Falls, Iowa. Did some "guest instruction";
1932 gave talks at Iowa State Teachers College, University of Iowa, and Indiana University.

1933 Spent part of winter in Des Moines and part in Altadena, California; the summer at Artists' Colony, Yaddo, Saratoga Springs, and at the MacDowell Memorial Colony at Peterborough, New Hampshire.

1934 *The Folks.* A Literary Guild selection.

1934- Residence in Washington, D. C. Lived for one year in
1936 Fairfax Court House, Virginia, while her husband was
connected with the Department of Agriculture for which
he wrote pamphlets and other material.

1936 *Carry-Over*. Appointed by President Franklin D. Roosevelt to membership on Farm Tenancy Committee of
which L. C. Gray was administrator and Henry Wallace
was head. Spent summer at Robert Frost's home at Shafts-
bury, Vermont.

1936- Lived in Cedar Falls; took active part in community life.
1938 During this time her sister's child, Judith Ann Hunting,
was married to Wells Barnett.

1939 Father died; buried in Cedar Falls, April 6. Ruth and
her husband traveled in Denmark, Norway, Sweden, and
England.

1942 *New Hope.*

1945 Associated with the University of Wisconsin Writers' In-
stitute in summer.

1951 Residence in Tucson, Arizona.

1952 Moved to Claremont, California. Purchased home which
she retained as her permanent residence until her death
January 23, 1960. After moving there spent part of one
summer and early fall in Moylan, near Media, Pennsylvania. Her husband studied at Pendle Hill. Affiliation with
Friends Society began about this time, but interest had
preceded this date. During World War II visited Civilian
Public Service Camps, units in mental hospitals, fire-
fighting units, starvation units under the combined spon-
sorship of the Service Committees of the Friends, Church
of the Brethren, and the Mennonites. She spoke on literary subjects, talked with young men and read manuscripts. *Some Others and Myself.*

1955 "Friends and Fiction" published in *Friends Intelligencer;*
review of *Robert Elsmere* in *The Georgia Review.*

1958 "The Surprising Anthony Trollope," *The Georgia Review.*

1959 *The John Wood Case.*

1960 Died January 23, Claremont, California.

CHAPTER *1*

Beginnings

R UTH SUCKOW'S BIRTHPLACE was Hawarden (pro-
nounced Hay-warden), a small town in northwestern Iowa
whose pristine quality she has made memorable both in the
novel *New Hope* and in *A Memoir*. During her growing-up years
as a minister's daughter, she lived in a number of Iowa communities ranging from small towns to middle-sized cities but
located in different sections of the state. She also experienced
rural life in visits to farmer relatives and in day-long excursions
to the homes of country people among her father's parishioners.
In all her fiction, Miss Suckow made use of this Iowa background. Some of the settings are identifiable. Besides Hawarden,
one finds the country around Manchester in "A Rural Community," and the college and town of Grinnell in "A Part of the
Institution." Most of the others are imagined composites; but
they are typical of Iowa even in their names, borrowed from
the map of Iowa, such as Belmond and Morning Sun.

Sinclair Lewis remarked that the fact that Ruth Suckow continued to locate her fictions in Iowa was fortunate for the state
inasmuch as her novels are "genuinely native."[1] It is true that
the state had never before received her kind of literary treatment, for Iowans Herbert Quick and Emerson Hough concentrated on pioneer themes; Hamlin Garland had an economic axe
to grind; and Octave Thanet (Alice French), although she employed Iowa place names, failed to convey the special Iowa
quality. But Ruth Suckow, like Sarah Orne Jewett in Maine and
Eudora Welty in Mississippi, deals simply and with great fidelity
with the commonplace material of the life she knows. As someone said of Gustave Flaubert, the result is not so much Realism
as reality. Readers of Suckow books come to know Iowa as she

knows it—the feel of its atmosphere, the lay of the landscape, and the intellectual climate and prevailing spirit of its people.

I The Family

The kind of little girl Ruth Suckow was is implicit in most of her fiction, for, in greater degree than the average author, she made use of the wonderful gifts of memory and recall that were hers. She was the younger of the two daughters of her parsonage home; her sister Ema (as she liked to spell it) was a vivid girl adored by Ruth; but, several years older, Ema moved in a different sphere of activity. Since the mother suffered from a chronic debilitating ailment, the rest of the family learned to depend on themselves. From *A Memoir* we gather glimpses of Ruth, a serious, very blonde child, playing with paper dolls in the window seat or whispering confidences to her companionable cat.

Ruth's father was accustomed to make his calls by bicycle, with a little seat attached to the handlebars so that he could take her with him. Like her predecessor Miss Jewett, who used to accompany her doctor father on his horse-and-buggy calls throughout the Maine countryside, Ruth absorbed much on these jaunts that she later used. Almost without knowing it, she was developing her acute faculties of observation. The feel of the fresh moist air, the spread of the land, the people's houses and their possessions, even the rhythms of their speech sank into her subconscious to become a part of that poetic appreciation for place that so distinguished her.

The Reverend Suckow, while always liberal in his views and by no means the heavy parent, seems to have influenced his daughter in significant ways. He was scholarly in his tastes and, although limited in training, had largely educated himself through wide reading. He never prescribed books for Ruth, who once said she read everything from *Pilgrim's Progress* to *Dottie Dimple;* reading simply came to be a constant and natural activity. And so it was with writing. Her father's book-lined study was Ruth's favorite room, and she was allowed to play there, if quiet, even while he was composing his sermons. These he wrote in large notebooks after his characteristically orderly habit. As a little girl she became accustomed to the process of composition—her father's rapt concentration, occasional mutterings, and movements as he pounded his desk lightly for emphasis. She herself was always a scribbling child, putting together tiny stories from her earliest years. She drew on fairy-tale lore, on other childish literature, and on her imagination, as in the tales she made up about her paper dolls. She liked to fold her compositions into little books and decorate them with her own drawings. Her script was small and neat—the forerunner of her later firm, vertical handwriting. One of these creations she presented to a favorite friend—one of the ladies of the church—with the hope that, though faulty, it would be acceptable "because it was original."

Like her father, too, Ruth Suckow was a truth-seeker and a truth-teller. She detested over-elaboration from her earliest childhood. As a mere youngster she discovered and rejected the falsity of the romantic happy ending. She respected profoundly the honesty of the realistic approach; she espoused it with enthusiasm and made it her own. But, if the father's gift to the young author was on the side of intellectual integrity, the mother's was preponderantly an artistic contribution. With limited means and forced by circumstances to move frequently from one parsonage home to another, Mrs. Suckow nevertheless managed always to make the house pretty to live in. She was an emotional woman, intensely ambitious for her husband and daughters; at one stage in Ruth's growing-up the young girl rebelled against her mother's "trying to live her life for her."[2] But in maturity the author realized the depth and burning intensity of the maternal love that had been lavished on her; and, as she said, her two parents stood equal in her memory.

II *The Communities*

Frank Luther Mott, an Iowa contemporary of Miss Suckow's, once listed the doctor's office, the newspaper establishment, and the parsonage[3] as the most advantageous situations from which to study Midwestern life of the period. Ruth undoubtedly gained much by growing up as a minister's daughter. She had an inside view of one of the most important institutions of the town—the church—and an interesting close-up of its members. Living in a number of different localities showed her how types of people tend to recur but at the same time have their own distinguishing features, just as each community, while resembling others in a general way, has its own character. Familiarity with the social rituals of the small town—its church programs, community picnics, and high school commencements—became part of her equipment.

To be sure, her vision was restricted to the doings of the "nicest" people in town—the church group and the civic leaders and their families. These families maintained a highly respectable front; if there were less savory aspects, they were carefully not discussed. It is possible that being a "nice girl" with obvious church connections may have sheltered the young observer and limited her subject matter when she came to write. Some of her critics have labored this point; one has even sighed for just a bit of "the meretricious" in her work.⁴ But Ruth Suckow was too honest a writer to introduce what, in her vision, was not there.

Another circumstance of the author's early years, resented by her at the time, possessed hidden advantages. As a member of a minister's family she was always somewhat detached, even from her companions; and she was not permanently rooted in the community as they were. It was as if an artistic distance were being fortuitously created for her; and moving about from town to town widened this distance. Because of not being completely identified with any one of them, she came to look at the various places where she lived in the objective way that is especially useful to a writer.

Just as Ruth Suckow was a member of the community and at the same time apart from it, she stood in a somewhat similar relation to the culture. Though both her parents sprang from immigrant German stock, they were completely Americanized, her father a minister of the church—the Congregational—most directly derived from that of the Puritan colonists. As a child, Ruth took particular pride in the historic tradition of this Church, for she was, she said, "a youthful American patriot and a very fiery one."⁵ She admired her church's stalwart simplicity and democratic organization as she saw them reflected in the plainness of the rituals and in the simplicity of the church architecture. Her favorites among the congregation were the old ladies of New England background whose firmness of character and austere refinement appealed to her. Later she connected their high thinking with Emerson and the Concord group—and she thought her father resembled Emerson in the cast of his features.

Yet her father, as was her mother, was German, not New England, and this German ancestry Ruth Suckow shared with a large proportion of Iowa's farming population. These German-Americans, however, engrossed in making the most of their new environment, undervalued their European cultural heritage and neglected the folklore, even the language, of their mother country. An exception was Ruth's grandfather whom she describes in a sketch called "A German Grandfather" in *American Mercury* for November, 1927. This old German, wearing his black cambric skull cap, gazed with a far-off look in his blue peasant eyes as he sang in German some of the folk songs from the "old country." In her childhood, Ruth's heart was touched by the gentle simplicity of this old man; but she allied herself intellectually with the descendants of the Pilgrims.

Many of these German-American relatives of the Suckows lived on farms, and her summer vacation visits in the country provided Ruth with another ambivalent look at her culture. Since Iowa had been at first completely agricultural, and since its small towns' sole *raison d'être* was to serve the farmers, the cleavage that exists between town and country in Miss Suckow's works is somewhat puzzling. Yet there was a decided rift, as Ruth's childhood experiences taught her and as we are forced to believe—a sense of superiority on the part of the town children that led them to draw lines against their country-bred neighbors.

But these only partially realized complexities in the life she knew did not at once clamor to be expressed, and as an adolescent Ruth felt drawn to another sort of artistic expression—that of dramatic or, as it is now termed, interpretive reading. This form of activity developed naturally from "speaking pieces" in Sunday School and grade school programs and was most congenial to Ruth's tastes as well as to her normal love of participating. In *Odyssey of a Nice Girl* she describes the high school "declamatory" or "oratorical" contest in which Marjorie Schoessel competes. Like Marjorie's, Ruth's talent was not oratorical nor highly dramatic, but a delicate lyric gift, enhanced by exceptional intelligence and sensitivity.

III *Schooling*

In her college years at Grinnell, Ruth appeared in a number of productions given by the dramatic club, of which she was an enthusiastic member. In her junior year these appearances culminated in her role as the fairy child in Yeats's *The Land of Heart's Desire,* a part her blondness and grace suited happily. Since she was active in Grinnell journalistic and creative writing groups at the same time (she majored in English literature), this participation in the Yeats play may have helped Ruth choose between her two loves, reading and writing. As a result, she left Grinnell at the end of her junior year to go to Boston to study at the Curry School of Expression.

A number of factors probably operated in this decision. Since Ruth had lived in Grinnell during her high school years, attending college there hardly held the glamour that "going away to school" had assumed in her dreams. She also needed to make a decisive break from her close-knit family who were reluctant to let her go. Boston had always held for her the allurement of far-off culture and tradition, and the School of Expression seemed to offer an open sesame to an exciting career. Inevitably, however, this Eastern venture proved a disappointment to the young Midwesterner. Living in Boston turned out to be a lonely and obscure existence, but she showed her firmness of character and remained at the Curry School for the two years required for graduation. She saw clearly, however, that elocution as a career offered no future at all for a poor young woman who needed immediately to be self-supporting.

As Ruth traveled west to Iowa and then to Colorado, anxiety on behalf of her family increased her burden of worry. Her mother was helping her married sister and young child locate in Colorado in what was hoped would be a health-restoring climate for Ema who had contracted tuberculosis. Ruth stayed on with them and entered the University of Denver where her experience was nothing like the Boston venture, which had been motivated by starry-eyed dreams of a career on the stage. Denver University was not even second choice—it was something available into which circumstances thrust her. Returning to her literary studies, she first completed the required work for the Bachelor of Arts degree and then as a graduate student worked toward the Master of Arts in English. She assisted Dr. Ida Kruse

McFarlane, head of the English Department, and taught classes
as a graduate assistant.

She was successful as a beginning teacher—a former student
remembers her "standing up before large classes of gawky ranch
boys and girls, a slender small person, talking with great sincerity of Walt Whitman and Thoreau"⁶—but she did not look
forward to a teaching career. Rather, her concentrated study of
literature reawakened her desire to write; for, as an underclass-
man at Grinnell College, she had contributed prose sketches and
a one-act play to the college magazine.⁷ Though obviously the
work of an immature writer, these show traces of characteristic
Suckow talent. One sketch, a monologue with gestures, humor-
ously portrays a fluttery co-ed about to try out for a part in a
college play. A short story, "The Joke," represents the rather
complex situation of an over-mothered boy cruelly snubbed by
his fellow students who regard him as a joke in spite of the
evidences of innately fine feelings and of literary talent that he
is beginning to display. "Miss Warrington's Burglar," a farcical
depiction of college life, is amazingly well put together; it features what was to become one of the author's favorite themes—
the conflict between generations—in this case the contrasting
views of an aging spinster and her niece.

Denver University supported no literary magazine in those
days; regrettably, no remnant from Ruth Suckow's apprentice-
ship as a writer remains in the university library nor in the
department of English. Not even a copy of her Master's thesis
(on women novel writers) can be found. But Denver contributed to her development in other clearly assessible ways. In the
first place, it opened her eyes to scenic beauty. Always a keen
and impressionable observer, she had learned to know and take
for granted the low-keyed agricultural vistas of Iowa. But in
Denver the grandeur of mountain scenery, spectacular and sen-
sational, spread before her view. And she spent summers in its
midst, working as waitress or chambermaid in the resort hotels
of the Colorado Rockies.

She had a friend, too, in those Denver days, with whom to
share her new experiences. Amy Carlson, an undergraduate and
somewhat younger, had similar tastes and ambitions. Now Mrs.
Aimée Buchanan, Amy has written entertainingly about a walk
from Estes Park to Denver with which the pair (without inform-

ing their familes, of course) wound up one glorious summer's work.[8] Though Ruth was small, she was utterly intrepid; and she guided and inspired the party of two through the considerable hardships of the several days' hike. Meals were often sketchy and lodgings even more so, but their souls feasted. Through it all, Ruth carried a small volume or two of poetry and her ever-present notebook.

IV Writing

Such confrontations of natural beauty probably account for Ruth's own efforts at writing poetry. She and her friend Amy were devoted readers of Harriet Monroe's *Poetry: A Magazine of Verse*, and ultimately they submitted some of their own work to that journal. Among Miss Monroe's papers in the University of Chicago library is the following joint letter from Amy and Ruth, but written by Ruth in her exquisite space-saving script, dated March 5, 1918:

> We have known you so long through POETRY that it will perhaps not be too presumptuous to ask for your advice. We are both in the University of Denver, one a "scrub faculty," the other a Senior. We both attempt to write—but we are so far away from the centers of writing and there is so little encouragement for original work in school life that we feel the need of help. Is it possible to teach school and write? Is there anything that a young and exceedingly unaccepted writer can do to earn a living and still keep on with the kind of work that she feels is her best? There are so few openings here—almost none but teaching and clerking. Is there any hope for one who is not in Chicago or New York?
>
> We are enclosing some of our work although we know that it is amateurish. If you will give us the benefit of your experience and advice, we will be very grateful.

Though Miss Monroe did not accept any of these first offerings, it is of interest that she wrote "Almost" beside Ruth's name. In 1921, *Poetry* published a group of four poems by Ruth Suckow[9] two of which, "Prayer at Timberline" and "Beauty," are obviously inspired by their author's love for mountain scenery. The poetry of Ruth Suckow, though we have so little of it, shows clearly the kind of artist she was to become. The verses are stripped and bare, like the trees at timberline; but each one has (to use her own phrase) that "singleness of emotional intensity that gives universality to the briefest lyric."[10]

At this stage in her life, as her letter to Harriet Monroe indicates, Ruth Suckow was chiefly concerned with finding a means of support while launching herself in a writing career. Keeping bees proved to be the solution of her problem. She prepared for it systematically by apprenticing herself to the woman beekeeper whose career she had read of in a Denver newspaper and by working hard to learn all its phases. Later when she returned to Earlville, Iowa, and her father offered financial help in establishing an apiary of her own, she was ready.

More important, she also was ready to begin her writing career. Her experiences in Boston and in Colorado had widened her horizons and had developed and deepened her emotional nature. In the East, she had suffered from loneliness, probably aggravated by remorse for having opposed her family's wishes. In Colorado, there was the disheartening progression of Ema's illness, the death of their mother, and then in 1920 the death of Ema's son, Robert Suckow Hunting. (Ema's death was to take place in 1923.) Grief matured Ruth Suckow. Added to her personal problems was her distress over World War I then raging in Europe. A conflict existed in her mind about religion, and this culminated in a disagreement with her father over what she conceived as the impossibility of reconciling Christian precepts with militarism. After her mother's death and the war's end, these differences were healed. She returned to Iowa with her father to begin her life as a writer.

In Earlville, the little country town where her father had accepted a pastorate, Ruth Suckow found the ideal location for her activities of beekeeper and writer. She established her apiary —she called it the "Orchard Apiary"—at a farm at the edge of town where there were numerous fruit trees and where flowers were raised for sale. She worked hard at it during the summer months and became successful. Mrs. Buchanan has described her indomitable small figure in enormous bee hat and veil as she lugged heavy frames and toiled long hours at the honey press. Moreover, she drove the truck to Dubuque to market her product.

Her home during at least a part of this time was a three-room cottage at the edge of Earlville where she lived alone in surroundings of bare simplicity. Untenanted now, the house still stands to suggest the austerities of an earlier day as well as the dauntless determination of the unusual girl who once lived and worked in it. Here she experienced the life of the rural country-side, the weather and change of seasons so crucial to farm work, and the intimate association with unselfconscious, hard-working farm people. She kept a journal during her first months there, and soon she began to write short stories. In Colorado, she had written poems; and one of these, published in the *Midland* in September-October, 1918, is often quoted:

> Heart, as shiningly wear your grief
> As frost upon a lilac leaf;
> As mist along the stubble rye,
> As silver rain across the sky.

Her early connection with *Midland* may have prompted her to send her stories to that publication. Her first three or four—among them her very best—were not only published in *Midland,* but led to an enriching friendship with the editor, Professor John T. Frederick of the University of Iowa. In *Borzoi* (1925), a collection of pieces by and about contemporary writers brought out by the Knopf Company to commemorate its first ten years of publishing, appears Frederick's" Literary Evening, Iowa Style." Ruth Suckow was at the center of the group he writes about, and he remembers her thus: "There was Ruth Suckow. Her clear skin was browned from days out-of-doors. She was small and cool and comradely. She talked genuinely and generously, and what she said crackled and burned with the fire of a tremendously vigorous intellect, ruthless and fearless, and yet tempered by profound understanding and sympathy."[11]

This sketch shows Miss Suckow at the beginning of her career as a recognized writer. At Frederick's urging, she spent her win-ters in Iowa City, helping to edit the magazine and lending the inspiration of her presence to the creative writing group he led. When Frederick, a protégé of H. L. Mencken, suggested that she send some of her work to *Smart Set,* Mencken welcomed her cordially and later helped her immeasurably with his encourage-ment and criticism. "He was like a kind old uncle to me," was the way she described the relationship to a literary friend and admirer.[12]

That the young writer had found for herself the art form that suited her best is evidenced by the rapidity with which she wrote. Beginning with the submission of "Uprooted" to *Midland* in late 1920, her stories poured out at the rate of ten or twelve a year; but they were also interspersed with novelettes and later with novels during a decade of remarkable productivity. Not only *Smart Set* and the *Mercury* but other magazines—*Harper's*, *Scribner's* and *The Century*—published her. She scarcely encountered a single rejection.

Late in life, Miss Suckow received from her publisher's agent a list of titles of her early short stories with a request that she check their publication data. She found herself in some difficulty. This sort of record-keeping had never interested her; she was constantly looking ahead, surveying possibilities for future work. After struggling with the list—"Mame," "Golden Wedding," "Uprooted," "Resurrection," and the others—she exclaimed, as if on impulse, "It seems incredible to me I ever wrote some of these things."[13]

The author did not explain her remark, and it must remain a somewhat enigmatic one. Possibly she meant only to comment on the inevitable dimming of memory with the passage of time. But to the student of her work, inclined to gasp at the plenitude and quality of this early output, it is of interest that the author herself confessed to finding something incredible about it. The genesis of the first stories, shaped from the samples of life observed, and acted upon by her own temperament, may offer some explanation; also to be reckoned with is the fact that she found her way into them by way of the lyric poem.

CHAPTER 2

Beauty

I went where pines grew;
Beauty I found in these,
In stars, and in the strange
Twisted boughs of trees.
I went where houses were;
Beauty I found then,
In eyes, and in the strange
Twisted lives of men.

THIS POEM by Ruth Suckow, one of a group of four published in *Poetry* in June, 1921, under the composite title "By Hill and Dale," tells us two things about the author—that beauty was all-important to her and that she found it in strange places: in the warped boughs of trees above timberline and in the lives of human beings who bear the marks of their struggles. Succinctly stated in the poem are the author's purpose, her chosen material, and her theme. In what is actually a statement of her creed as a writer, beauty is named as her objective.

I *Journal*

Upon her return to Iowa to begin her writing career, Ruth Suckow found herself deeply moved by the charm of the natural scene around her. This homely rural landscape that she had always known was unpretentious with its fields and pastures, its red barns and white frame houses. Over it arched the wide sky, the clouds cast their shadows, and the seasons wrought changes. Small, reticent beauties lurked for the careful observer —a single golden tree or clump of half-hidden spring flowers. Into her journal went impressions of these, together with her compulsion to give them form and permanence. She wrote:

"Beauty that must be kept/And held, must have a mold."[1] And "If I go out seeing, feeling, having words rise to my mind out of all the beauty like bubbles out of whirling water—and do not write them down, make the mold!—the day goes bitter, sick, fruitless."[2]

There was more than a touch of surprise in her responses. After the Colorado mountains, how could one find an Iowa pasture appealing? She wrote: "O loveliness of my world of beauty —mountains, swamps, and aspen valleys—all incomplete without this vision of early spring sunlight in the Iowa fields."[3] In another place, she recorded that "One does not need mountains, waterfalls, shining places. I think I love beauty even more when it is half imperceptible like this—nothing but a road and a sky, the smell of evening, and birds singing in the bushes. Then beauty is only a little part—a sign—of the something overpowering in nature."[4]

The journal entries are not all devoted to the physical scene, for a natural story-telling bent often asserts itself. She tells of a dog that followed her on one of her late winter rambles to the top of a muddy hill. Written in free verse in a conversational style remindful of Robert Frost, this narrative concludes as follows:

> I rather think that I've met that same dog since,
> But we always pass each other.
> He never gives me a narrowed look—"Now isn't that the
>   girl—?"
> He knows what humans seldom know—
> That a thing is when it is,
> And then it's over.
> And so we keep that moment on the hill intact—
> That satisfaction of black earth and aging snow—
> And never talk about it.[5]

It is obvious that the young writer was finding human nature her ultimate concern. The "strange twisted lives of men" are seen to have their own kind of beauty. Her neighbors in Earlville are the subject of reflections. Such a character as little Alec Prentiss, for example, whose fondness for a strange plant, like a green rose and called "life everlasting," sets her speculating.

In her poetry-writing stage, Miss Suckow had written a piece in free verse about an elderly woman, almost a recluse, who devoted herself to the care of her flowers and trees. Under the title "An Old Woman in a Garden" this very early poem was published in *Touchstone* in 1918. It bears a striking resemblance to certain of the author's subsequent short stories. Beginning in this characteristic fashion:

> People say
> That she must lead a lonely life,
> With that empty house
> And that great lawn,
> So set apart from everyone. . . .

it continues with her answer:

> Why not?
> I've known folks all my life.
> It's time I was making friends with other things—
> With earth and rain and flowers.
> They'll be all I'll have soon.

She must have realized after writing this poem, however, that prose was better suited to her material. "An Old Woman in a Garden" is a kind of bridge between the lyric poems that were her first literary expression and the short stories that she was soon to write.

II *Early Short Stories*

All these early stories are low-keyed, with a note of sadness. They deal with somber themes—death and illness, poverty, deprivation, old age, and loneliness. Of the sixteen that were later gathered and published in *Iowa Interiors*, all but three or four are about old people. Because of these subjects, critics often commented that Miss Suckow chose her subjects from the unlovely aspects of life. Yet, paradoxically, the purpose which motivated her was to grasp a moment of beauty and preserve it. The beauty she perceived and that she again and again celebrated is appreciated the more keenly as the circumstances are seen in their unadorned reality.

To Ruth Suckow, with her uncompromising honesty, to "prettify" was to desecrate. If life is truly beautiful and worthy to be loved, she seems to say, its quality should be tested by the everyday situations and not by the unusual ones. She says something like this in "Great Days," a passage of free verse that is in her journal:

> Great days should mean great happiness. But they have never
> Been what they promised to be. Perhaps the heart
> Grew strained in its high expectancy, like the string
> Of my violin that I stretched too tight in my eagerness
> And that gave off a note with a wailing echo in it.
> There is this about them—to great days I look forward
> But seldom look back upon them. What I look back to
> Are sudden haphazard days as unexpected
> As the shining flight of a gold finch across the road.
>
> Days when I came upon fields, or little quiet houses,
> Exquisite outlines of trees, and flowers—or only
> Days when suddenly out of the air around me
> A glory came upon me stronger than sunlight.
> The glory comes of itself, like beauty, and loving,
> And no great day can win it by preparation.
> So perhaps I will be very wise, and give up all striving
> For the great days—but will only go quietly letting
> Myself come upon a day that is sweet as a wildflower,
> Or let a day come upon me, like meadowlark music.
> Perhaps the great days have been great too long; and perhaps
> It is time to take a new path, or cut across country,
> So I may find the freshness and the glory.[6]

In choosing her subject matter, Ruth Suckow deliberately took a new path—that of depicting everyday people in the hampering circumstances of day-to-day existence. Later, after her stories and novels had won for her a secure place among practicing authors, she was often asked to address writers' conferences. Among her notes for one of these talks is a mention of the purpose that impels all writers. She puts it in the words of Lady Murasaki who in *The Tale of Genji,* an eleventh-century masterpiece, disclosed that novels are written because of something in life that has so impressed the writer, either for good or evil, that he wants others to know about it. There must never come a time. she feels, when people shall not know about this. It is too valuable ever to be lost.[7] So Ruth Suckow herself must have felt about the glimpses of "freshness and glory" she caught now and then, unexpectedly, in the lives around her. She taught herself to perpetuate these impressions in a form she thought worthy, so that people might know about them and so that they might last.

The early stories have a lyric quality. Some are very short: "Retired" is six pages; "The Resurrection," five. They present a situation, make it recognizable by actual details from its setting, breathe life into it, and let it stand, a messenger of beautiful truth, like a poem. The elements of nature are used to convey and intensify meaning. In "A Home-coming" and in "A Rural Community" this imagery is more elaborate than in the briefer stories. Nature is often used to set a mood—the bleakness of a cold rainy day pervades "A Start in Life"; the urgency of incipient spring makes itself felt in "Retired."

Though the stories move through time toward a crucial moment, they tend to be more pictorial than dramatic. Sometimes the moment is frozen into immobility by some device such as the taking of the photograph in "Four Generations" or the look on the mother's dead face in "The Resurrection." Some are epiphanic like those of Anton Chekhov whom Miss Suckow much admired. Often a cumulative effect is built up from a series of random happenings as in "Renters" or "Mame," or from a patterned sequence as in "Golden Wedding." Though the stories are simple, they show a surprising variety in method. The narrator is frequently objective, but occasionally she moves inside her central character's mind, and when she does, she renders thought into appropriate speech patterns with great naturalness. There is never any evidence of experimenting. In each case, the method exactly fits the story, as if the inspiration had brought with it its own manner of telling.

The situation in "The Resurrection" is sketched with a few simple strokes—the grandmother is lying dead in the parlor, and the family is summoned by the undertaker to view her body, now prepared for burial. Her beauty and remoteness startle them all. The littlest grandchild thinks of the transformation wrought by frost upon the familiar world of outdoors. Her daughters, used to their unobtrusive, hard-working mother, are moved by the unexpected grandeur of her presence. But the climax is her old husband's half-dazed recognition that, through the mysterious power of death, this strange loveliness has emerged—the spirit of her virgin girlhood, which only he among all who now behold her has seen before. Dimly he perceives that he has witnessed a resurrection; then he sinks back to everydayness as he comments to his granddaughter, "Your grandma looks—real nice, don't she, Nellie?"[8]

"The Resurrection" has an almost stylized precision about it. Yet its very starkness suggests depths of emotion beneath. Many years later, in "A Memoir," the author spoke of looking upon her own mother's face in death: "My mother's face, young and beautiful as I could never remember having seen it, marks of her long illness erased and the best look of her lovely young girlhood come back."[9]

"Four Generations," mentioned above, is essentially pictorial— the taking of a family picture in which, as the title indicates, four generations are represented: the old German grandfather; his son Charlie, a prosperous Iowa banker; Katherine, Charlie's daughter, home on a visit from the East; and her little Phyllis, the great-grandchild and center of the group. The group is thrown into brilliant relief by the brightness of the hot July sun on the deep green of the grass and the snowball bushes which form the background. Interest focuses on the four figures brought to life by skillful touches—Grandpa's frail hands clasping his knotted stick, Charlie's luminous bald skull, the tense cords in Katherine's neck, and little Phyllis's delicate arms, damp with the heat. Off at the side other family members draw back against the house, careful "not to get in the picture" (248).

Actually the picture *is* the story. It is external, but revealing. The sequences of interior monologue only bear out what the picture itself suggests: Charlie's baffled resentment at the distance between himself and his only daughter and grandchild; Grandpa's disappointment that he has nothing to say to Charlie, now a "town man," not a farmer; and Katherine's shrinking from the "feminine grossness" of the women's conversation, as she contrasts her relatives with her husband's family and their New England ways that she feels actually closer to now than to these Iowa ones. The final scene rounds out the piece—pictorial once more, but this time with sound—as Phyllis, up from her nap, approaches her great-grandfather as he sits quietly smoking in the doorway of his small house. Like an inquisitive bird, she hovers, draws back, approaches tentatively. To lure and keep her, the old man speaks gently, quizzically: "Is dis a little yellow bird? Can it sing a little song? No? Den Grandpa will have to sing one to you." And he quaveringly sings the old German folk song "Du, Du, liegst mir im Herzen" (261).

The symmetry of this work, together with its vivid picturization, gives it an exquisite unity. It is far from slight, however; it suggests a number of themes central to Miss Suckow's thinking and reinforced in her later works. The four generations, so close together in the opening picture (the photographer keeps urging them to move closer), are actually divided and torn apart by differences. The conflict between town and country is here, that between Eastern and Midwestern culture, the German versus the New England tradition, and the never-ending strife between the generations. The final scene resolves the paradox as great-grandfather and little grandchild draw together. The rifts and resentments that trouble those in middle life mean little to the very old and the very young; they hold in common their love for the fundamentals of simplicity and beauty.

"A Home-coming" conveys its meaning through the flower imagery that suffuses its descriptions. A flower fancier, Ruth Suckow nowhere shows her indigenous quality more truly than in her accurate knowledge of what blooms and when in Iowa gardens. Even the place names in "A Home-coming" are suggestive of flowers. The town is Spring Valley; the street is Summer Street; and the girl, no longer young, who returns to her home there is named Haviland, suggesting the fragility of pretty china, often flowered. Not much happens in this rather leisured story—it is situation merely—but the flower symbolism gives it poignancy.

Laura Haviland has spent her best years traveling about with and waiting on her restless, demanding mother. Now, the mother dead, she has come back to find everything changed. The town has adopted new ways, her home shows the effect of long neglect, and her childhood friends are now brittle matrons. The pathos is in the drained vitality of Laura, who cannot find the zest either to make a new life or to adjust to the changes of the old one. She is like a wilted flower, her hands supple but lifeless.

In the back yard of her old home, once full of flowers, there are only fallen petals of the syringa, their scent bringing a thought of Mark, the lover she relinquished long ago. The grass under the catalpa tree is sprinkled with white ruffly blossoms edged in sepia, tacitly suggesting the wedding gown unworn and her own wasted flowering. A lone wild violet left blooming she greets with a soft cry, "Darling—beautiful." But there are no "spring beauties" in their old place by the little cobwebbed cellar window (33).

Wistfulness, gentleness, and flowerlike fragility give this story its special tone, but without its confrontation of evil it would remain merely sweetly sad. The evil is selfish maternal domination, which the author represents in a metaphor of force and violence that yet remains perfectly in keeping with her chosen imagery of plants and flowers:

> She thought of herself at twenty, when her mother and she had left the first time for Florida. How she had felt aching, bleeding, *as if she had been torn up by the roots.* How she had said to Mark: "We will certainly be home in the spring." So they had—and then had had to go again. Her mother's need of her *creeping about her like tendrils, fastening on her and holding her tight.* She had said to Mark: "I feel . . . it isn't fair to you" and his always unbelievable acquiescence. That same year he had married a girl from Fort Weston . . . (34). (Italics mine.)

Now Laura has come to realize that what she has been born for is not hers. Nothing is hers except the old house, the trees, the fallen petals on the lawn.

"A Rural Community" also shows a character, this one a young man, who returns to his native environment. In contrast to most of Ruth Suckow's Iowans, Ralph Cheney is, like the author, a writer, a traveled person, hence one capable of making comments in his own voice; and the tone is reflective and poetic, rich in symbolism. Ralph's return takes place in the autumn, and many of his impressions resemble the author's journal entries for that season: "One slender young cottonwood, yellow as a goldfinch and as lyric in its quality, stood in a meadow, alone" (160). The glowing and transient colors, seen against the unchanging landscape, point up the tension between change and permanence —the dominant impression of his visit. The remembered line of hills on the horizon reminds him of the eternal verities, suggesting the stability that he misses in his transient life. Another kind of permanence, that of human personality, is expressed by his old foster mother, who exclaims on recognizing him: "It's the look in your eyes—I'd have known ye anywhere" (163).

Ralph's foster parents mourn that he has no wife and that his newspaper work takes him to all corners of the world. Gazing at the display of family photographs in the parlor—weddings, first babies, then family groups with children growing up to engage in the same unending cycle—the wanderer recognizes the difference in the point of view of these rural relatives: "Human relationships were what they understood, the things to which they clung" (175). But Ralph's fate is not so tragic as Laura's fruitless life—it is only rootless—and he suffers merely a mild nostalgia at the sight of familiar scenes.

When he takes the night train for the East, he feels that his visit has done him good: ". . . All night long, as he lay half sleeping, swinging lightly with the motion of the train, he was conscious of that silent spreading country outside, over which changes passed like the shadows of the clouds across the pastures; and it gave him a deep quietude" (183-84). The play of the ephemeral shadows over the everlasting rocks of the pastures is a revelation that speaks to Ralph's soul and serves as the key symbol of the story. Natural beauty serves in a transcendental way to represent that "something overpowering in nature" that the author writes of in her journal.

In another of the stories, "Retired," nature speaks to the inner consciousness of man. Seth Patterson, an old retired farmer, on an early spring day ambles down town on an errand for his wife, drops in at several places along Main Street, exchanges small talk with cronies who hang out at the produce store, and in the late afternoon trudges back home. On the first warm day in March everything suggests planting time to Seth. "Won't be long now till the ground's ready," he mutters (133). Though Seth is at loose ends and discontented with his aimless life, feeling, as he says, "crabbed and helpless, sitting around just gassing with the ground getting soft and the sky blue" (136), his story does more than point out the need for educating for retirement and old age. His response to the vital urgency of the day with its scent of melting snow, fresh mud, and bright clean air indicates a mystical partnership of man with nature.

Seth Patterson represents a special kind of attainment. His reaction to the March weather is proof of what his kind of life has made him—he is inarticulate, wordless as the forces of nature themselves, but he is acutely aware of them and perfectly attuned to their call. In his own way, the old farmer is completely at home in his world. To attribute futility to such a life, as some readers have done, is to misunderstand the meaning Miss Suckow has so carefully planted.

In "A Start in Life" natural conditions provide a metaphor for the cold, unsympathetic world. The weather is rainy and bleak as twelve-year-old Daisy Switzer goes to work as a hired girl for a promised dollar and a half a week. Ironically named (she is a homely little thing), she suggests a straggling flower beaten down by the rain. There is a chill about everything in this story— the bare, clean, new little house; the cool, offhand treatment of the young Kruses in their determination not to make Daisy one of the family. "You must help me," Edna reminds her. "You know we got you to help me." The coldness affects Daisy, for children, even the not-very-sensitive-ones, like Daisy, suffer when there is nobody to care about them. As the rainy twilight sets in, Daisy sadly sees the truth of what her mother has told her: "This isn't like visiting" (2).

"Renters" projects a similarly pessimistic outlook for the Mutchler family. Echoes of Hamlin Garland sound in the hopeless frustration of the hard-working husband who is turned off the farm he has made prosperous by owners who now see the place as a desirable haven for one of their relatives. "They expect a man to take care of it like it was his own," Fred says bitterly, "and then any time they can send him off" (129). He goes on: "What's a fellow gonna do? He works and does the best he can with the land he's on, and then they want it for someone else. And if he don't work, he has to leave. He has to leave anyway. There ain't nothing in it for the renter. There's nothing unless a fellow owns the land he's on" (130-31).

His wife Beth has thoughts even more corrosively cynical: "Fred made her angry. Under the savage bitterness of some of his words there was always that something appealing, something childish and ready to trust people, in his eyes. Oh, he was a good worker and he was honest, but it needed *something more than that to get ahead. Something hard was what it needed.* Old lady Hunt had it, and Mrs. Foster showed it in that bright, glittering, mean smile she could turn upon you. *Why wasn't Fred like that?*" (130).

Though Miss Suckow pays some attention to the injustice of

"the system" as it affects individuals like Fred Mutchler and Daisy, she is for the most part concerned with "universals"; and the short story "Mame" illustrates this concern. There are touches of fatalism here. Mame and her husband Alick have always been unfortunate, and the rest of the family says it does no good to help them. "Why did there seem to have to be one like that in every large family? All the hard knocks and none of the good things. Why did life seem to have it in for folks like Mame?" (85).

But sociological explanations of their problems are of less concern in this story than the nature of Mame herself—she is self-sacrificing (almost too good-hearted, the brothers agree). She has looked after the younger children and has stood by her Alick whom she insisted on marrying after the accident that left him crippled. Mame and Alick moved into the old home to care for her parents through their old age and final illnesses. Mame has always put her own welfare after that of those she loves. Now that her plight is becoming desperate because Alick is too lame and feeble to work and because the small country town offers few opportunities for her and her daughter to earn money, she has appealed to Louie, the brother she feels closest to, to drive over from his home in the county seat to discuss what can be done.

Nothing is done, as it turns out, beyond Louie's giving Mame a check for twenty dollars to meet overdue payments on her sewing machine. This is one of Miss Suckow's masterly delineations of a situation which is left unresolved—but its very insolubility reveals the strength of the forces set against each other. Louie, a prospering businessman, suffers from his own ambivalent feelings—grateful affection for his sister who he knows is "the best and truest among his brothers and sisters," and selfish inclination to follow the lead of his wife and his other relatives in avoiding involvement with Mame and Alick's problems.

The physical objects in the old, run-down house where Mame and Alick live contribute to his mixed feelings. He is impatient with the doors that won't catch, with the rocking chair that threatens to capsize: "Didn't these people ever fix anything when it was coming to pieces?'" (75). At the same time, everything reminds him of the old days, his sister's unfailing goodness, and the fact that "he never felt at home anywhere else in just the same way as here on this old familiar lounge with Mame" (83). Mame's solicitude for him—"You look kind o' thin, Louie" (72)—shows her readiness to turn from her own troubles to thoughts of others. Ineffectual though she is, Mame's character is the bright touch of beauty in this all-too-human struggle between head and heart that Louie epitomizes.

"Golden Wedding" is another example of Miss Suckow's treatment of universal themes cloaked in the specific details of a recognizable situation. This account of the fiftieth wedding anniversary of an old Iowa couple takes them through the winter day just as it happens: the trip in the bobsled to their daughter's farm home, the big dinner attended by all the relatives, the sleigh ride in the afternoon, the taking of photographs, supper, and finally the return to their home and the resumption of their everyday existence.

The old wife's consciousness illumines the narration. Throughout the perfectly rendered incidents and embedded in her reactions are indications of a long-standing conflict of personalities:

> Why did Pa have to be so mean—and just today? He wouldn't admit that the celebration would be held in spite of the snow-storm; he never wanted to admit that anything was going to turn out right. But she still held to this blind faith of hers, and he to his objections. She pulling ahead, he pulling back.
>
> And that old tie he wanted to put on, just because, as he said, "Nobody would want to come out in all this snow just to eat dinner with us." He wanted to tarnish the glory of the occasion—pull it down to his level. The old tie was a blow at her importance as his wife—at their marriage—at her pride as a bride of fifty years. (264)

However, as the events of the day rise to their climax, old Mrs. Willey feels her faith justified. The presence of the minister elevates the family dinner to an occasion. The table is decked with the best silverware and table linen that the family can boast; the food is sumptuously beyond the ordinary. She and Pa preside at the head of the table, she cuts the cake, and Pa even makes a speech. In the gaiety of their after-dinner ride through the snow in a sled decorated with the slogan "Just Married," he goes so far as to raise aloft their clasped hands to signal passersby. As the celebration dwindles to its end, though, the commonness of everyday asserts itself, and Pa resumes his usual stance.

He only grunts when she attempts to relive the events of the day in bedtime conversation. As she lingers over the putting away of her best clothes and trinkets, he orders her crossly to come to bed. "Pa would never talk to her," she mourns. "He'd talk more to anybody than to her" (282).

"Golden Wedding" takes its form from the traditional Prothalamion, a celebration of the ritual of marriage from the donning of ceremonial attire in the early morning, through each observance of the day to the disrobing and union of the wedding night. But the ceremony is manqué—defective. Not all its poignancy resides in the travesty of re-enacting in age and disillusionment what was once made beautiful by youth and hope. Here, as Miss Suckow would say, particularity has its importance, too.

Old Angie Willey is more than merely the bride figure. She has a life of her own, shaped by her kind of environment, and conditioned by fifty years of intimacy with a tenaciously opposed personality. Hers is the immemorial quest of the self to know and fulfill itself; and in this quest, marriage in general and her marriage partner in particular have worked against her. "She pulling ahead, he pulling back" is the way she puts it (262).

Her old husband, though harsh and insensitive, is not entirely the villain of the piece; their life of narrow conformity is much to blame. Angie's spiritual gropings can find no expression beyond the clichés of the local paper, and her innate love of beauty has rigidified into a pinched regard for seemliness. Undeniably, she is warped and frustrated, though no more so than many another old person on whom life has inflicted its hard teachings. As an individual with thoughts of her own to cherish, she ends her day in finding contentment within herself.

"Uprooted," Miss Suckow's first published story, still stands as one of her very best and as an exemplar of her philosophy about the writing of fiction. This philosophy she was later to discuss in magazine pieces—"I Could Write if Only"[10] and "The Short Story"[11]—and in talks at writers' conferences. The details in "Uprooted" serve not only to set the tone or to provide background for the narrative, but also to perform a part in the resolution of the story. The Shafer "relationship," three married children and their spouses, gather at their parents' home to decide who is to "take" the old people, now no longer able to live alone. The action takes place in the parlor, described with the most specific realism—musty air, old photographs, flowered carpet, doilies tied to the chairs with ribbons, illustrated Bible, and all— and in the bedroom where the old mother weeps at the prospect of being separated from her "things," and where Sam, eldest and best-off of the family, persuades her to move in with her daughter by promising that she "can take everything in the house if she wants to"—he'll build on a room to Hat's house if necessary (103).

The amount of enmity, jealousy, and self-protectiveness underlying the discussion in the parlor almost justifies an early critic's judgment that Ruth Suckow's works principally succeed in showing "the petty selfishness, the vicious current of hatred which dominate human intercourse in the corn country.[12] Sam controls the situation because of his financial standing and also because he is his mother's first-born and her favorite. But he is not allowed to settle everything without some struggle—with his acerbic sister-in-law Jen, his obstinate if inarticulate sister Hat, and even his mother herself, whose withered person, pathetic in the tearfulness of old age, rouses some remnants of filial tenderness. There is ironic humor in his middle-aged businessman's eagerness to get through with all this and go home to the comfortable leather chair "whose hollows are his own" (97), while at the same time he tells himself impatiently, "How strange it is that people seem to take root in a place!" (106).

The outcome of the story is pessimistic, even cynical, in that the burden of caring for the old people is foisted on the one least able to bear it because she is also least adept at protecting herself. Heartache is foreseen for the old parents; that they are already aware that they can no longer control their future is indicated by the mother's bitter words: "They've fixed it among 'em" (105). The author's purpose, however, is not limited to ironic commentary. The compromise on which the settlement hangs involves the mother's "things," so dear to her that she will not consent to abandon them. At the beginning, they are meticulously described, one by one, in a way remindful of Huck Finn's description of the Grangerford parlor a half-century earlier. Looked at in this light, the doilies and knick-knacks are pure Americana—genuine bits of local color. They also set the stage for the action, a fitting background for the family conclave taking place in their midst. Graceless, materialistic, yet eminently respectable, the character of the Shafer family is reflected in the primly placed, decorous furnishings.

They serve to illustrate a deeper meaning. The author remarks: "Those things were all about him now," as Sam paces about the parlor after settling things with his mother. "He could not look at the pampas grass sticking up absurd and stiff from the blue painted vase. The elaborate lace curtains tied back with cords of red plush, the sea shell beside the door, the ingrain carpet, musty smelling, and patterned all over with great sprawling cornucopias of roses—his muttered "Oh, pshaw" betrays his softened feelings as he half turns to the bedroom to repudiate his decision. Then he shrugs and puts the impulse from him.

At this point the furnishings act as mute reminders of family ties. The room where they stand is a shrine, seldom used, but representative of family solidarity and status. As Sam dimly senses, the old home-maker who has long cherished these articles feels more than affection for them—her very life is bound up with them. Instinctively, like an uprooted plant that can survive in its new place only if packed and cushioned by its own soil, she insists on surrounding herself with the same familiar objects she has always lived with. Finally, in their power to participate in and affect human destiny, these things are raised to a certain momentousness. They have almost the stature of a protagonist in the working out of the story. The author's genuine feeling for concreteness has made possible a happy harmony between the physical setting and the characters, or, as she would put it, between localism and universality.

Later when this story was gathered with the others into *Iowa Interiors*, critics were quick to liken them to the works of the Dutch genre painters. The precision of detail and the luminous clarity of the Dutch interiors, it was often pointed out, were the very qualities the Iowa writer achieved in her word paintings. Of all the stories in the volume, "Uprooted" owns the most apt affinity with the title. In her concern with domestic scenes, the author presents a number of interiors done with meticulous care; but on none has she concentrated the passion of attention she gives the Shafer parlor.

The name of the collection has a symbolic bearing, of course. It is plain that Miss Suckow meant her interiors to be the same ones that Hawthorne had in mind when he coined his famous phrase in connection with his masterpiece: "the interiors of the human heart."[13] Mencken's review of the book in his "Library" section of *American Mercury* (November, 1926) caught this purpose of the author with fine discrimination:

In Miss Suckow's stories situation is usually of small significance; the salient thing is the anatomizing of character. Who among us can manage that business with greater penetration and understanding, with a finer feeling for the tragedy of every day, with a more moving evocation of simple poetry?

. . .Who indeed, at home or abroad, has ever published a better first book of short stories than this one? Of the sixteen stories, not one is bad—and among the best there are at least five masterpieces. I mean by masterpiece a story that could not imaginably be improved—one in which the people are overwhelmingly real and not a word can be spared. All of these people are simple Iowa peasants. In other hands they would slide inevitably into stock types, ludicrous and artificial. But Miss Suckow differentiates them sharply, and into every one she breathes something of the eternal tragedy of man. Her talent is not unlike Sherwood Anderson's, but her mind is more orderly than his. She gropes and guesses less and is hence more convincing.[14]

Quests

INTERSPERSED with the jewel-like short stories that Miss Suckow produced with such plenitude in the early 1920's were three examples of a form she always favored—the short novel or novelette. Sinclair Lewis, who considered her *Country People* as also belonging to this genre, named its author among the masters of this "swift-winged form," as he called it.[1] Toward the end of her life, Miss Suckow mentioned in a letter to a friend that she was "absorbed in writing some long short stories" which she hoped might eventually make a small volume. She commented that she found the form "beguiling," though "that length of story is difficult to place—it seems to fit nowhere."[2]

These early novelettes, which came out in *Smart Set* between November, 1922, and October, 1923, resulted from the same creative urge as the short stories; and they have the same poetic genesis. Though their greater length poses difficulties, Ruth Suckow's art is equal to sustaining their unity of impression and their singleness of emotional impact. In each case she takes a single character as a focus of interest, and one dominating trait is traced throughout almost the entire life span with the effects and outcomes it brings. With admirable control, she never deviates from this central concern, though scenes and incidents are fitted out with a wealth of imagined detail.

As Miss Suckow indicated to her friend, her editors showed some reluctance to accept these longer pieces. Nathan reminded her of the magazine's general limit of fifteen thousand words but conceded that " 'A Part of the Institution' is good enough to make any magazine editor break his rules."[3] The decision to feature them as "novels complete in one issue" was a fortunate one since they are actually fairly short, between twenty-two thousand and twenty-five thousand words.

Favorite themes of Ruth Suckow are treated in these three stories. *The Best of the Lot* deals with sacrifice, the familiar situation of the unmarried daughter spending her life and energies in family duties and the care of elderly parents. *Other People's Ambitions* presents another Suckow concern, that of tyranny, one human being victimizing another for selfish aggrandizement. *A Part of the Institution* is a semi-satirical treatment of the small denominational college of the Middle West; its theme is the pitfall of false or weak idealism. Because these novelettes have never been reprinted and so have not received the critical attention they probably deserve, they need to be examined in some detail.

I   The Best of the Lot

The Best of the Lot, which first appeared in the November, 1922, issue of *Smart Set*, is a simple account of the life of Jennie Robinson, a little country girl who devotes herself to her shiftless family, slaving to raise them to respectability, insisting on standards of behavior and education for her brood of brothers and sisters, all of whom are ordinary. Though Jennie achieves a measure of success with them for a time, it is at the cost of sacrificing her own chance to marry. Later, she gives up her humble teaching career to care for her aging and invalid parents. The brothers and sisters, selfish and indifferent, leave home early, abandoning Jennie to a state of neglected poverty. At length, after her mother's death, she is left completely alone in her elderly house. Now a quaint little spinster, her energies and ambitions drained, her only outside occupation is keeping up the family graves in the cemetery.

Though Jennie reminds us of Mary in "The Daughter" and Laura Haviland in "A Home-coming," she is as she should be in this lengthy work, more fully realized. We see her grow and change throughout the years. Engaging glimpses are given of her—small, neat, and industrious as she flies about the hotel dining room where she works, little beads of sweat glistening on her forehead and upper lip. She conscientiously admonishes her little sisters: "No, no, Jennie says no. Nellie knows better."[4]

Of the three novelettes, this one is the most indigenous. Descriptive passages are true to rural Iowa. There are touches of beauty in the commonplace scenes. The Robinson children play out in the grove, described as follows: "They would spend whole hours there, in the green leafy dimness, where they could just hear the sounds from the road. They picked wild flowers, wild gooseberries, raspberries and chokecherries, May apples and butternuts. The grass was long and fine, marked with the faint shiny tracks of wagon wheels. They lay on their backs and watched the leaves move against the blue sky" (9).

More than the other two, this novelette is a forerunner of the novels to come. The opening farm scenes are similar to some of those in *Country People;* for example, there are the little frowzy-headed country children whose mother has too much to do. The earlier Jennie with her furious energy and ambition, her ability to organize her family, resembles Cora in the novel of that name. Jennie's brother Charlie is an embryonic Carl (later described in *The Folks*), whose conformity is at war with his better nature.

As in the short stories, Miss Suckow relies on generalized comment to round out her characters and set the tone. "People said: 'I guess Jennie Robinson hardly knows what to do. I wonder what she lives on'" (36). Jennie's relatives and the family doctor expand the comment. Doc Zimmerli says: "I'd take Jennie any time. The best of the lot, too good for the rest of them" (36). Though scrupulously detached as always, the author reveals compassion for Jennie. Her sacrifice is made to appear admirable, but there is regret for the seemingly useless waste of excellent human material in unrewarded and unappreciated self-abnegation. Like a number of the short stories, this novel closes with a puzzled and unreconciled protest against the way things are. As Doc puts it: "It was queer how the ones that deserved the most got the least half the time in this world" (36).

Dreiser's influence and that of other contemporaries in the school of Naturalistic determinism are felt in this work. Early in the story occurs this statement about Jennie's parents: "The two breeded like animals, without volition or knowledge of any kind, not wanting more, but accepting the warning of another with a worried sense of fatality" (6). This bluntness is not typical of Miss Suckow. It departs from her usual reticence, doing violence to her policy of "staying out of the story, of letting the characters live."[5]

Ruth Suckow's apparent desire to register protest against things as they are also strains the credibility of this novel.

Though misfortunes and the selfish neglect of the rest of the family make a victim of Jennie, one feels that she lets down too easily: that the indomitable Jennie of childhood years would not turn into the passive, inhibited old maid she becomes. Though facing destitution, she lacks initiative to do anything for herself —she even shrinks from peddling a line of toilet goods among her friends and neighbors. Jennie did well in college, yet later her intellectual life seems insufficient to sustain her or to suggest means of escape.

The same objections could be raised as to Mary's limpness in "The Daughter" and to Laura Haviland who, though still in her thirties, lacks energy to resume living her own life after her mother's death. The fact that Ruth Suckow herself suffered from physical inadequacy in her middle years comes to mind. But, to look a bit deeper, Jennie and the others she resembles seem doomed by their own self-sacrificing natures. They can give unstintingly of themselves for others but not for themselves. That their weakness may be the result of a subverted maternal impulse is not understood by the possessors nor by those around them.

Their society approves the sacrifice of these maiden daughters and encourages the mothers to expect it. As Miss Suckow wrote, with some asperity: "Most of these widows had once been farmer's wives with enormous families; and each one had providentially one daughter left to her for her sole benefit. It was so nice for the mothers, everyone said sympathetically. 'Such a comfort to her that she has Mary.' These women had led the average lives, with the average mixture of pleasure and joy in their sorrows; but still it was felt that, as women and mothers, a 'comfort' was due each of them" (30). The daughters, on their part, respond both to the prevailing mores and to their own inner promptings to tenderness in caring for their helpless parents. "She felt as deep a loyalty, a responsibility, to her mother as she would have felt to her child," is said of one of these sacrificing women in an early short story by Miss Suckow.[6]

II Other People's Ambitions

Although Mencken and Nathan both warmly admired *The Best of the Lot*, Nathan expressed reservations about the next novelette, *Other People's Ambitions.* He wrote: "Your story, 'Other People's Ambitions,' pleases us, and we are accepting it. While it does not seem to us to be quite so good a piece of work as *The Best of the Lot*, it still contains an ample measure of excellent writing."[7] The editor does not explain his statement, but one can guess that he missed in this novel the Iowa background Miss Suckow was in the habit of re-creating with such effortless authenticity. Most of the action in the new novel takes place in Denver, which the author also knew well; and it must be said that her close knowledge of sanitariums and the peripatetic health seekers that frequent them is capably utilized. But the familiar setting in Iowa is lacking.

The main character in this work is a young man, Harold Swisher, the son of a wealthy and domineering Iowa manufacturer. Harold, a graduate of a liberal college, is opposed to the career in the family industry envisioned for him by his father, tries it for a year, and suffers a physical breakdown. After a stay in a Denver sanitarium, he regains a measure of health and determines to remain in the congenial Colorado climate and live the kind of life he desires. His father, after helping him obtain a not-too-strenuous job that would maintain him, declares he will do no more for him and leaves him free to follow his inclinations. Harold's future looks fairly hopeful in an unspectacular way when May appears on the scene.

May's situation is that of one of Ruth Suckow's not-so-young maidens devoted to the care of her widowed mother, but with a difference. This maiden is designing and determined, and she sees in Harold a means of achieving married status and a home that she can dominate. She snares him without great difficulty when her mother's death heightens his sympathy toward her, and the two begin their version of love in a cottage.

After a short idyllic interval, during which May revels in organizing and decorating the house and Harold dreams of a life of continued beauty and leisure, their cross-purposes become plain, and May shows herself a more formidable tyrant than Harold's father. A selfish materialist rendered acutely unhappy by others' good fortune and possessions, she nags her husband continually. She longs for the luxuries of apartment dwelling, better cars and clothes, a standard of living that to her spells success. She keeps at Harold to exert himself to make more

money, to secure a higher-salaried position, to induce his family
to shower them with luxuries. He is able to resist her for a time—
the birth of a child satisfies her restlessness temporarily—but she
is the stronger of the two; and, though he is aware that his health
will suffer, he yields to her urgings. They leave behind their
peaceful, half-rural existence; he attempts a more strenuous,
less congenial type of work, worries about it, and sickens. His
early ailment reasserts itself, this time with more virulence, and
in a few months he is dead.

Superficially, this plot resembles that of a dozen slick magazine stories. The domestic wrangling between husband and wife,
May's specific wants, the detailed descriptions of their way of
life, their house, car, and, later, their baby—all are familiar. In
her skill in presenting domestic details like these, Miss Suckow
resembled popular women's magazine writers of her time. She
had a sure understanding of feminine nature together with an
overweening love for the concrete appurtenances of daily living
—"the things of use and wont," to quote one of her most laudatory critics.[8]

Miss Suckow's works differ from typical magazine fiction, however, primarily in her basic attitude toward her material—an attitude quietly but unmistakably manifested. In this novel she is
deadly serious. Harold and May are locked in a death struggle,
not a frothy married lovers' dispute. The fate of the individual
forced to yield to other people's ambitions is extinction. Irony,
rare in the regulation "slick" story, is also implicit in the assump-
tions of the other characters about Harold. His sisters complain
that he will not do as other people do. He is queer from the
start. In college his cronies are a Professor Quarton and a mousy
girl named Quigley, (the initial "Q" is indicative of their queer-
ness). The life Harold desires for himself is a modest existence
with leisure to cultivate and appreciate beauty. To his relatives
and May, this is no life at all; and they assert that he lacks ambition. But the title betrays the distinction between the ambition
of these others and Harold's vision of life which is beyond their
abilities to conceive.

The word "ambition" in the title is perfectly chosen. To Miss
Suckow's Midwesterners, it possessed connotations closely tied
in with the prevailing system of values. "Ambition" was a highly
favorable term implying a whole list of virtues; outstanding

among them was the proclivity of exerting oneself to the utmost of his powers—"to work till he dropped." In that society and in that era, leisure was discredited; it was equated with idleness and closely associated with dissipation and evil. Buried somewhere in the meaning of ambition was also the ruthlessness necessary to achieving material success, a hardness akin to cruelty that would not brook interference. Ruth Suckow's people did not advocate cruelty, but they accepted it as an ingredient of ambition. The end justified the means, and the aim of life was "getting ahead."

Harold, who has felt the brush of dark wings in his collapse and during his sojourn in the sanitarium, knows the futility of the dream of "getting ahead." His own dream is different. Others discredit it and he is not allowed to realize it, but it is a not less worthy dream because of that. On the contrary, its difficulty of attainment even implies something of its loftiness. In the best sense, Harold is the truly ambitious one after all.

Other People's Ambitions resembles regulation magazine fiction in its organization and plotting, and it is tighter and smoother than many of the author's other works. The struggle rises to its climax in a series of engagements between the protagonists, subsiding between times to stretches of everyday existence under a sort of armed truce. The narrative is crisp and clear, like the Colorado atmosphere; and it lacks the nostalgic overtones of Ruth Suckow's Iowa pieces. It furnishes an indication of the kind of writer she might have become had she more often ventured into worlds she knew less well: shallower, perhaps; more obviously fictional; but possibly even more acceptable to the popular taste. But she is less herself, and surely less poetic. Nathan may have had something of this in mind in his unexplained reservations about *Other People's Ambitions*.

Needless to say, the ending of this novelette is completely at odds with the happy ending expected of magazine fiction. Indeed, the off-beat quality of its conclusion is at odds with most fiction, breaking sharply with the rule against dragging in new characters and situations at the close. But Ruth Suckow always insisted that her kind of stories obeyed no rules except their own.[9] In this one, she seemed to feel the need of a commentator on Harold's tragedy and sketched her in, complete with her situation, so that the final paragraph is an entire little short story in itself.

> . . . .The wife of the president of the seed house [where Harold worked], a discerning woman, made thoughtful by ill health which had forced her out of social life, had only touched his life at the outskirts. But she thought of it, wondered about it. It was one more note in her bewilderment concerning the world— why it should have been. The whole story, as she had had it from her husband and had made it out for herself, was one of those things whose existence she simply could not understand. One of the things that made her suddenly look at her husband, with his pink, kindly face and neat little optimistic definitions of life, with sudden, wondering, alien eyes. (37-38)

III   A Part of the Institution

The dominant note of *The Best of the Lot* is pathos; that of *Other People's Ambitions* is tragedy. But that of *A Part of the Institution* is satire. Hester Harris is another of Miss Suckow's self-abnegating old maids; but we have to smile at her mistaken devotion, for the object of her love is not another human being but an institution of learning—little, self-centered, self-satisfied Adams College. Hester can not escape her fanatical loyalty to Adams. She was born and bred in Adamsville, in its shadow; her mother is a distant connection of its founding family, and Hester's childhood home is a rooming house for women students. College activities absorb her interests from the beginning; the co-eds are the heroines of her dreams. She prays to grow up a popular, "all-around" Adams girl. In time her hopes are realized. Blessed with a singularly sweet smile and a nature marked by willingness to serve, she is recognized as a true "Adams type"— one thoroughly imbued with Adams ideals.

In Miss Suckow's analysis of Iowa earlier referred to, she writes of the "milk-and-watery idealism" in the colleges of the state, particularly the denominational colleges.[10] At Adams, idealism is implicit in the student-body prayer meetings, in the powerful influence of the Y.M. and Y.W.C.A.'s, and in the missionary spirit which yearly impels a number of students to volunteer to carry the Adams spirit to benighted countries. But the flaw exists in the emphasis on conformity—the pressure on individuals to adjust to the group pattern. The conformity most favored consists in joining all campus organizations of prestige and, through energetic and faithful membership plus political finagling, working into control of these. It is expected that active, "all-around" students will wear themselves out in extra-curricular activity (some literally kill themselves), but the sacrifice is highly regarded as being made "for dear old Adams."

Hester performs as a true Adams co-ed. Her successful four years in college are marred by only a slight defection when during her junior year she falls in love with Joe Forrest, a quiet, rebellious boy who dares to question the worth of the Adams ideals. Hester ardently tries to make a convert of Joe; but when she fails and he is suspended, she flees back with something like relief to the shelter of the group and resumes her active campus life with zeal. Her friends have followed her affair with Joe disapprovingly; they feel he is "not the person for her." But when he is gone, there is nobody. Though Hester is a prominent senior, she has lost her chances with the popular Adams men.

After her graduation, Hester's desire to serve, to devote her life to promoting Adams ideals, traps her into accepting a poorly paid "scrub faculty" position at the college. For a time she throws herself into the ungrateful job with eagerness; then she is needed to help with a special endowment campaign; eventually she becomes one of the president's assistants, a "part of the institution," whose old-fashioned mien earns her the ridicule of younger office girls and the contemptuous nickname of "Hetty G." Reduced to existing in housekeeping rooms with her failing mother, she lives in anticipation of the reunions with her classmates at commencement times. The final glimpse of her is after one of these, bidding her old friends goodbye on the station platform of Adamsville. Mature, worldly, and successful, they respond to her eager affection with a pitying fondness she only partly understands. Obviously, Hester is the perpetual college student, one not very different from the character in Irwin Shaw's "Eighty Yard Run," reliving the glory of his achievement in college football. Hester, too, has failed to grow up. She is the victim of her college successes, when she represents the perfect embodiment of the group's ideals.

Miss Suckow's presentation of Hester is knowledgeable but gentle. Hester is silly in her unthinking devotion to Adams and in her pleasure in her popularity as a campus figure; but she is nevertheless warm-hearted, hard-working, and loyal—richly endowed with the feminine traits of a successful wife and mother. She should be part of a family, not of an institution—the very word reflects the coldness, the barrenness of poor Hester's fate. The institution has exploited her, utilizing her sincerity and unquestioning devotion in poorly paid, drudging work. But even Adams College is gently dealt with. A nostalgic glow surrounds the buildings, the trysting places, the college pranks, the good times, and most of all the young people themselves. Bunty and Ellen, Jinny, Joe, Big Bill, and Jay are amazingly vital individuals, full of high spirits and shining with youthful promise. Like the later *New Hope*, the Adams community has Utopian qualities of freshness and faith; but the ideals on which it rests are weakly defined and readily adaptable by hypocritical selfseekers.

In *A Part of the Institution* is found some of the best writing in the novelettes. There is no sentimentality, but warmth and understanding pervade it. The satire is light, inducing many a smile. There is naturalness in the speech patterns, for example in the child Hester's fervent prayer, "Make me like my darlingest, belovedest Helen and be taken into EBB—if it pleases Thee that I should—but, oh, *please* dear Heavenly Father because I can't bear to live if I'm not," and her mother's admonition: "Darling, mamma likes to see you good, but you make such long prayers when it's so cold. Your little feet are like ice. Can't you do part of your praying in bed?"[11]

The description of the hot Iowa summer when Mrs. Harris and Hester shut themselves in their darkened house and wait for fall to bring back coolness and life to the town is at the same time utterly realistic and also symbolic of an existence narrowed and circumscribed, dependent upon one agency—the institution: "That summer seemed endlessly long and dull. Hot—every day worse than the one before. The nights were terrible. Hester and her mother did not pretend to do regular cooking. After a little lunch, they each took a bath, put on their nightgowns, and tried to read and sleep in the darkened back parlor until the worst heat of the day was over....The town was nothing without the college people. How could she ever stand it until fall?" (20).

There are other examples throughout this work of style and content wholly in harmony. The large trees that droop over Hester as she walks away from the station at the end convey the author's sure feeling for Iowa atmosphere as well as regret for the futility of Hester's wasted life: "Humphrey had left her. Her steps seemed loud on the wide cement walk. The tall elms stood up thick-leaved, motionless, as they would all through the long hot summer, throwing gray dappled shadows on the asphalt. There was that after-commencement feeling—a growing languor, a sadness and a uselessness in the fragrance that floated out over the thick, moist, solid, mid-June heat" (53).

IV Country People

There is reason to believe that Miss Suckow offered *Country People*, her first novel, to *Smart Set* for publication just as she had her short stories and novelettes, and that Mencken suggested that she publish it in book form since it was too long to appear in a single issue of the magazine; he felt that dividing it would spoil it. He had earlier suggested that she publish a novel before collecting her short stories into a volume, assuring her that the public reception would be more cordial to the books in that order. The novel that she was working on and that he asked her repeatedly about was almost certainly *Odyssey of a Nice Girl*. Its length and complexity, in contrast to *Country People*, indicate that the author hardly regarded *Country People* as a novel at all. As her husband once remarked, it was written in a surprisingly short time, without agony or revision; seemingly, the work was the result of a unified burst of inspiration.

Yet *Country People* is an achievement notably beyond the novelettes. Larger in concept, as it is in length, the novel portrays an entire family—in fact, four generations of one—made up of varied personalities who respond differently to an environment which changes strikingly during the chronicle. The work can be considered as the record of the culture—a subculture, really—of the German immigrant settlers of Iowa and their descendants. During the lifetime of the main character, August Kaetterhenry, the Iowa frontier develops into the prosperous state of the 1920's, and its German-American settlers are completely absorbed into the farming community. What gives unity to this extensive undertaking is its author's conviction, stated in her analysis of the Iowa culture, that these very country people—the substantial, practical, materialistic farming population—give Iowa its special character.[12]

Country People tells the story of the Kaetterhenrys, August and Emma, who in the first sequence start out as young people; progress in the second to the position of substantial landowners; meet in the third the problems of wartime and their retirement from the farm; and finally succumb to old age, illness, and death. This account, more like a case study than an epic, presents the early struggles of a young couple beginning life on their farm, coping with numerous children and the care of ailing parents, laboring to "get the farm paid for," and then gradually achieving a cautious prosperity. Changes in their living conditions are made clear through such concrete details as the furnishings of their house, modes of transportation, farm buildings and equipment. Social life is described through church services, holiday observances, courtship and marriage customs, and relationships between parents and children. Nothing beyond the ordinary run of life happens to the Kaetterhenrys; they merely experience what hundreds of farmers of the period experienced.

The novel, of course, ceases to resemble a case study when the protagonists emerge as real people. Miss Suckow, always closer to her women characters, allows frequent glimpses of the thoughts and feelings of Emma. She is gentle, self-effacing almost to a fault, timid about asking August to bring things from the store, and inclined to submit to the domination of her difficult mother. She worries about Johnny, the wild one of her children but her favorite. She cherishes the memory of the trip to Rochester which culminated in her operation and considers it a high point in her life. As a widow, in the closing years of the chronicle, she exhibits a faint flowering of personality—a capacity, though undeveloped, for appreciating the simple beauties of her existence.

August is treated with greater distance, but he obviously stands as the model of a successful German-American farmer. Though Emma has no easy time of it, she knows it is true, as her relatives tell her, that "she has a good husband." He has enormous driving energy and stubborn persistence. "He's one of the best workers around," people say of him (56). Strong and durable himself and lacking in imagination, he has little tolerance for weakness in others; hence, he has only a modicum of kindness and gentleness. His appreciation for non-material values is nil; he scorns those who treasure such values (his father-in-law and his oldest daughter Mary) as dreamers. Yet he prides himself on his standing as a church member: "To him, going to church, and being steady and a good worker, and not drinking, and paying his bills, and saving money, were all part of the same thing" (155). They are the rules he lives by; otherwise, religion means nothing to him.

Because his virtues of thrift and orderliness, industry and persistence, coincide with the requirements of successful farming, August becomes a respected member of the community. What other people think of him is ritualistically expressed at his funeral and in the obituary published in the local paper at the time of his death. "Esteemed citizen," "conscientious farmer," and "honest and upright man" are some of the honorific terms. His neighbors respect him because he has built up a well-improved farm worth a substantial amount of money, because he is a director of the bank, because he has retired with sufficient means to build a solid house in town and live there in comfort—in other words, they respect him because of what he has accumulated.

But Miss Suckow throws occasional light on the inner life of even so impervious a subject as August. He is baffled and angry but hurt, too, at being reviled as "Boche" and "Old Dutchy Kaetterhenry" during World War I. Wasn't he born here? Wasn't this his country too? (108). And during Emma's illness he suffers—faces a blank void at the thought of losing her; and when she recovers, he treats her with greater consideration. Always upright, August lives according to the mores of his society. Why then the sadness and bareness he feels about his new house when it is finished? He can't explain it. He can't enjoy the comfortable life in town that he has worked so hard to achieve.

Emma also wonders after August's death, about this problem, as she returns from visiting her father, old Grandpa Stille, at her sister's farm:

> Emma thought about it as Carl was driving her home between the September fields of dusty gold in the late afternoon. She could still hear those faint, far-apart, devout German words. August had always said that if her father had been more of a farmer and less of a preacher, he'd be better off today. August had despised him in a dispassionate way. But the old man had had something, she hardly knew what, that had lasted him when his work was over.

[54]

"He's got something to think about," she thought.

It was that something, she could not name it, which she had missed all her married life.

She remembered the pathos of August, coming in from the farm and saying bitterly that everything had to go Carl's way now; of him sitting about the house, trying to look at the farm journal, not knowing what to do with himself. Her father, what a frail man he had been when he first came to live with them years ago! And here he was living still, contented with the little that he had, and well, and August was the one who was gone. (197-98)

Country People, like many of Ruth Suckow's early works, was misunderstood at the time it appeared. It left questions—dissatisfactions. It granted the validity of the American success formula, based on hard work plus the resources of the country, as it worked itself out on the fertile farmlands of the Middle West. But then it questioned the outcome. What was the meaning of the glibly mouthed term "success"? The human factor would not fit passively into the formula. There were both Kaetterhenrys and Stilles to be considered, and even the Kaetterhenrys felt longings for something beyond material prosperity.

A number of critics attributed their discontent with the book to its curiously flat, impersonal tone. They felt that Miss Suckow's dependence on generalized narration was a mistake. The author's first mentor, John T. Frederick, disagreed with "her notion of how a book about country people should be written."[13] He believed that what she produced was too bare a chronicle. Certainly her determination not to involve herself in her characters' feelings left them isolated in their inarticulateness so that many readers found them at best colorless, or at worst grotesquely cloddish. Her country people are illiterate German peasants whom she presents in their unadorned reality, refusing to act as interpreter for them herself or to tell their story through a friendly narrator. Her approach differs from that of Willa Cather, who handles similar material by manipulating her point of view so as to surround her main characters with a glamorous haze. Those who enjoyed Miss Cather's stories about Bohemian or German settlers in Nebraska, and who found them fresh and appealing as seen through Jim Burden's eyes in *My Antonia,* for example, were uncomfortable with the Kaetterhenrys. They seemed too *primitive,* and it was felt that the author's manner also had a touch of the primitive.

Miss Suckow herself, upon rereading *Country People* for inclusion in *Carry-Over,* a collection of some of her previous work brought out in one volume in 1936, decided the novel had held up well. She thought that it contained "a certain amount of bedrock" and that the style in its "careful country minutiae, its touch of dry country humor, even its hardness and tightness" was appropriate to the material. She described its narrative style as having the low, monotonous music of a windmill.[14] It *is* low-keyed, unmelodious throughout; for the choice of words is limited as nearly as possible to the language of her characters; the sentence structure is kept to the simple, declarative form a foreign speaker would use; and the text is flavored with occasional dialectal expressions from the German.

When August, threshing at the Stille farm, first sees his future wife Emma, the narrative, an approximation of his own thoughts, is framed in a series of short, simple statements that express his hard-headed calculations: "He liked her. He wondered if she was pretty strong. She seemed able to get through with a lot of work. She did not look in the least like her mother. She was a giggler; both she and Mollie could seem to giggle by the hour, but just the same she was pretty sensible. She taught country school in the Benning Township schoolhouse, but she knew how to wait on threshers" (36).

When he sees Emma next day, "He pretended not to notice, but he saw the girls, standing there leaning against each other, half closing their eyes against the sun, which was bright on their black hair and flushed cheeks, the blue dresses against the blazing gold of the straw-stacks and the stubble under the blue prairie-sky" (37). This type of fairly long sentence set among habitual short ones is one of Miss Suckow's favorite patterns. Copious participial constructions enable her to paint a colorful little scene, a vignette, not exactly in August's words, but just as it impresses itself on his senses. It was the evening after this sun-drenched vision of Emma, rather than following his common-sense appraisal of her, that August "cleaned up" very carefully, although usually he "didn't think it was much use until threshing was over" (38).

Emma's hesitant, conciliatory personality—as well as the ever-present conflict between generations—comes through in the way she tells her sister, "Ach, I don't know. Ma has her old ways of doing things, and the children don't seem to like what she makes" (75). Later, when she herself is a grandmother, her simple enjoyment of the quilting afternoons in the church basement is indicated: "There was the crisp smell of coffee, which some of the ladies were getting ready on the oil-stove, coming in and saying, 'Well, don't you ladies think you better quit working so hard and have a little coffee for a change?'" (158). In this vivid scene, rendered in a single sentence, with heavy reliance on participial structures, the women's speech has a true folk quality; one feels that the archness of the references to "working hard" and "for a change" are about as close as they ever came to humor in their pleasantry.

Emma shows herself a Stille, not a Kaetterhenry, when she putters in her garden in the spring. She enjoys raising flowers; they are food for her sense of beauty.

> She liked to be out there planting in the spring. . . . It was silent and sunny, no sound but an occasional car on the road, a rooster crowing, sometimes the noise of Junior's little kiddy-car on the cement walk. She liked the feel of the cool spring earth, sun-warmed on the surface, black and moist and chill underneath, as she patted it over the tiny dry seeds. She talked to Junior, said, "Dig over there in the corner, Junie, if you have to dig too, then"; but her mind was far away from him, in some wordless place of mysterious content. (207)

The author's closeness to Emma is revealed by the fact that she feels no need to explain her by means of the communal report—"People said—." Instead, she closes her novel with an exchange of confidences between Emma and her neighbor, another elderly widow whose husband, too, has been a farmer. After the two women discuss such intimate matters as operations, final illnesses, and family problems, Mrs. Wall tritely suggests that they have much to be thankful for. "We don't have to be sent to the poorhouse like that woman in Bishop," she reminds Emma. Emma's reply, with its unmistakably German accent, has the low-keyed music of the windmill: "Ja, that's true, too" (213).

Country People may be favorably compared with Pearl Buck's *The Good Earth* which, as a matter of fact, it somewhat resembles not only in its substance, which is the wresting of sustenance from the soil, but also in its method, since both novels contain an inspired adaptation of the vernacular of the characters, one rendered with an almost scriptural simplicity of vocabulary and sentence structure.

V   Odyssey of a Nice Girl

Odyssey of a Nice Girl is one of those novels that every novelist seems to produce once: a book devoted to the childhood and adolescent experiences of the main character. They are often stories of quests, in which the individual seeks to find himself, to answer the question "Who am I?," and to adjust to the world as an adult. Since these books are legion, their interest must develop from the unique quality of the individual seeker and the nature of the difficulties encountered.

A fairly long book, *Odyssey* is literally crammed with details. A letter from Mrs. Alfred A. Knopf to the author, written after her first reading of the manuscript, indicates that in its original form it was much too long and would have run to two hundred twenty thousand words when only ninety thousand words would be sufficient to "get this girl between covers."[15] In the same letter she praises what Miss Suckow was attempting to do, called parts of the book "simply glorious." But she urges the young author to take six months and cut the work; in its final form, *Odyssey* seems not to have suffered from the cutting.

This sort of book gave scope to the author's vivid memory and her exceptional powers of re-creating place and period. Before writing *Odyssey,* she had sketched some notes for a similar work about a little girl in a small Iowa town. After her death, her husband Ferner Nuhn submitted a portion of this unpublished work to *Midwest,* the literary review of the State College of Iowa, under the title "A Little Girl's World," with the following prefatory comment:

This fragment is apparently the start of an unfinished early novel by Ruth Suckow. It is written in the tiny neat script of the author in a very large notebook, really a scrapbook, whose first few pages have pictures of eminent people pasted on them—selected, it would seem, by the writer herself as a little girl. But the writing evidently comes from the years in which Ruth Suckow was finding her way as a novelist. She spoke of the effort to write a book about this little girl as something "which did not come off" but from which "she was able to salvage something. . . ."

This fragment . . . has a certain completeness. It reflects the love of places, the savoring of detail, the wonderful powers of recall which Ruth Suckow possessed, together with its special evocation of the world of childhood.[16]

Many of the details of places and persons in this fragment are identifiable with those of *Odyssey.* The houses and places of business in the small town, minutely described in both works, indicate Ruth Suckow's special gift for evocation through the mind of a child; and so do the children's activities, their personal loyalties and rivalries and their dreams, hopes, and fantasies. In *Odyssey* the wealth of detail not only tends to obscure the theme of the book but also prompts a doubt as to whether the re-creation of this child's world in love and nostalgia is not after all its real purpose.

The title, however, serves in part to dispel this doubt. *The Odyssey of a Nice Girl* suggests a quest and at the same time the quality of the quester. *Odyssey* indicates a prolonged wandering, directionless at times, and often diverted from its goal by perverse forces. Like Ulysses, Marjorie is in a sense seeking for a "home" where she can be herself, a happy and fulfilled individual. As in the case of Ulysses, a marriage companion is essential to that complete fulfillment. The qualifying phrase that describes Marjorie implies that the difficulties of her search are due in part at least to her being the sort of young woman Iowans of the World War I era and before spoke of as "nice."

Marjorie is "nice" in all of its many meanings. She belongs to a "nice" family, church-going and substantial. Her father is the son of a German immigrant farmer, as was August Kaetterhenry; but Ed Schoessel moved to town and became a furniture dealer and undertaker. Her mother, who is eligible for the Daughters of the American Revolution, is thought to have condescended a little to marry Ed. The Schoessels have money enough for the ease and comfort of "nice" living, even for a modest aspiration to gentility, with pretty clothes for Marjorie, membership in clubs, and music lessons. When we first see Marjorie at about nine years of age, she is carrying a little ruffled parasol and boasts of owning a China silk dress. "She had the prettiest room of any girl in town" because her father owns the furniture store.

"Nice" girls conform to a pattern. They are agreeable and well-mannered. In Buena Vista, the social arbiter is Mrs. Phillips, a large-busted matron with pretensions to culture. When Marjorie and her friend Neva are asked to serve at Mrs. Phillips' receptions, it means that they suit the prescribed pattern as to appearance and behavior. "Nice" has also a specific meaning connected with a girl's relations with boys, but in Marjorie's case, and possibly in that of most nice girls, parental control is so rigid that this distinction may well be taken for granted. Except for a short-lived flurry over a high school basketball player, she spurns local boys but dreams of a tall, fair-haired athletic young man like those in books, whom she will meet in some faraway, romantic place. Finally, Marjorie is nice in the word's older sense—fastidious. (Her family calls it being "fussy.") A natural outcome of the pampering she has received, her niceness is also a deeply rooted characteristic: a feminine delicacy of taste inherited from her mother and her aunt Bessie Blossom. This quality is less than endearing as she scorns the plainness of her paternal grandparents' farm home, but it serves to keep her uncorrupted by the cruder elements in her environment.

Because of the fortunate circumstances of her early life, Marjorie believes that she is destined for a fate beyond the ordinary. As a child, her daydreams of the future are synthesized from her reading; she sees herself presiding over a gracious Southern mansion like those in the *Little Colonel* books, marrying an English lord, and having afternoon tea and dressing for dinner. As she begins to grow up, her music seems to offer special meaning and beauty, but later she turns to dramatic reading which has always held an appeal. After she excels in a high school contest, she entreats her parents to send her to Boston for advanced study at a school of expression.

Like her author, Marjorie succeeds in winning only a reluctant consent from her parents. Also like Miss Suckow, she is disillusioned by many aspects of the school. But she gains in maturity from being in the city and develops confidence in her individual taste in literature and performance. She has a slight but authentic talent for interpretation—the "lyric gift," as her teachers call it, inspired by certain works of delicate sensitivity such as the poems of Christina Rossetti. In her final appearance at the school

of expression, as Titania in *Midsummer Night's Dream,* she feels
she has reached a peak of achievement that momentarily satisfies
her inner longings.

Marjorie plans to go on to New York with her friend and fellow student, Emily, but she meets opposition from her family
that sweeps her backward like Ulysses. Her mother writes:
"No doubt New York would be very interesting to be in. But
papa and I both feel that we have spent all this money giving
you your training, and now you should make use of it. Papa says
he does not see what you could get to do in a publishing house
and certainly after all the lovely training that you have had you
do not want to be a clerk. Are you sure that Emily has the very
best influence over you?"[17]

The provincial tone of this communication suggests what
Marjorie has to contend with in her struggle to find a niche
where her slender talent will fit. No one in Buena Vista recognizes her for what she is—only with difficulty has Marjorie herself won a partial and negative self-knowledge. She knows she
can not read the "cheap things" from James Whitcomb Riley that
the home audiences clamor for, nor play to the audience by
melodramatic tricks or by giving readings with musical backgrounds. The small perfection she is capable of is not in demand.
She is still floundering in a sea of uncertainty when she returns
to Buena Vista.

Her year at home is dismal, marked by an offer from a girls'
school in Mississippi, a position she wishes to take in spite of
the meager salary of five hundred a year and board and room.
But her parents remonstrate, her mother exclaiming "It's much
more backward down there. Mrs. Phillips says that in some
towns in the South they don't even have city water and have to
drink rain water. Anyone as fussy as you are, Margie, would
never stand that!" (268).

Marjorie is not, however, to be understood as the victim of
parental domination, nor even as the "nice" but colorless product of small-town mores. These influences only hinder her development—the real struggle is engaged in within her own nature.
The ambivalence of her desires pulls her in opposite directions.
She dearly loves her home, both because of the comforts and
niceties of its living arrangements and because of the reminders
of her happy childhood that make it meaningful to her. Yet, on

the other hand, she needs freedom to fulfill herself as an individual. In the provincial boundaries of her environment, such freedom is impossible.

After an interval, Marjorie breaks away again, this time to Chicago on the pretext of taking a physical training course to augment her speech specialty; but she is intent on finding a job to maintain herself permanently in the city. Though the job proves to be only typing and filing for a small hosiery firm, and the salary insufficient to provide the kind of living she desires, she is at last self-sustaining. About to achieve a sort of victory, she is called home by her mother's illness. Tossed back into home waters again, she learns that one of her basic needs is being needed. "No job mattered beside mamma," she decides. "People came first." And "she knew that she was happier at home than anywhere else, when she was needed, when there was actually a reason for her being there" (286).

Her mother recovers, but then the war comes, and after her brother's enlistment and death, the care of a little nephew gives her an excuse for staying at home. Though some of her friends find in wartime activity an avenue of escape and self-expression, Marjorie is out of sympathy with the waves of militaristic enthusiasm that sweep the town; her integrity will not let her use the war as an outlet for her own ambitions. After the war, she sinks into depression; rallies after a minor operation; and, as spring comes, feels again her old needs clamoring to be fulfilled. She seeks freedom from the hampering house in walks in the countryside, finding even in the tame Iowa scene something fresh and beautiful. "She longed to possess this beauty, not just feel it" (315). When her father becomes ill, she accompanies him to Colorado, finds herself responding to the different scenery and freer way of life. After her father's death, she finds the strength to tear herself away at last, and she returns to Colorado.

This is the real end of Marjorie's Odyssey; the final section is an epilogue in which she does not appear. Mrs. Schoessel, on a visit to her old friends in Buena Vista, tells of Marjorie's marriage to a war veteran in Denver and the couple's plans to settle on a fruit ranch. Much discontent at this ending of the novel has been expressed. It has been pointed out that the changed point of view (after it had been Marjorie's throughout) gives a chopped-off effect, almost as if the protagonist had died. There is not enough "drama" in Marjorie's final step to give the outcome significance—the forces do not engage with sufficient violence. And the lack of momentousness in her commonplace marriage has seemed to many readers to reduce the meaning of the entire quest. In her mother's words, "If it was all to come to this in the end, anyway, why couldn't Margie have been content to marry Chub Patterson and let them all stay in Buena Vista?" (362).

Examined in the light of the author's purpose, however, the structure of *Odyssey* has its own suitability. The details that seem over-plentiful, even random, are in reality carefully selected for their cumulative effect, like those in the original *Odyssey*. They are piled up, repeated, and skillfully described until they convey a sense of actuality. The irony of the title is that whereas the Homeric stage props are purposely vast and impressive—giants and Cyclops and puissant storms—in the Suckow novel they are minute, humdrum, and domestic, like the cistern cover where Marjorie liked to sit and dream in the shade. Ulysses' is a man's life of daring and confronting great things; Marjorie's is a woman's, cherishing little ones.

Throughout the narrative, Marjorie's author scrupulously maintains one point of view—Marjorie's. Not only is hers the only center of consciousness, but the events are related in her words, colored with her feelings; and her thoughts and impressions are conveyed as nearly as possible as she would convey them. This achievement is notable since Marjorie's powers of self-analysis and self-expression are feeble and could easily have reduced her story to inconsequential dullness. But always Miss Suckow's employment of just the right detail serves to illuminate her material. The very quality of Marjorie's love of home, for example, is seen in her appreciation of the freshness and daintiness of the Schoessel kitchen, "even the dishes on the drain-board, steaming from the hot rinse water that ran down into the white sink" (227). All Marjorie's reactions are intrinsically feminine ones. This femininity, though delicate, is so frankly revealed that one masculine reader, when the book first appeared, exclaimed: "A man really ought not to be reading it!"

Miss Suckow's treatment of the outcome of Marjorie's quest is also fitting, since her heroine's final and courageous act is tearing herself away from her old home. Not violent in a superficial sense, her going without a backward glance at the tree house or a parting word to her old dog Buster is a torturous wrench for Marjorie. Similarly, her telling herself that "She simply had to plunge on now . . . and then slowly, after a long, long time, perhaps things cleared away"—inarticulate as it is—represents the culmination of her long wandering. To the understanding reader, Marjorie has reached her goal. All that follows is anticlimactic and is properly presented as a sequel, in someone else's words. Marjorie's mother is the right choice for this reporting, for she has been closely associated in the search, not always understanding but always warmly loving. Her interpretation of Marjorie's course is what one would expect of her—provincial and limited, but ennobled by selfless affection.

The commonplace marriage is recognized as Marjorie's true destiny, for she, after all, is a simple girl whose desire for a place of her own to be herself, and for someone who will appreciate her for herself, is a natural one. Her arduous quest is necessary because too much pampering has kept her a little girl, and has given her false notions of the kind of future she deserves. She is not ready for even her undistinguished destiny—she has to earn it. What she learns from Emily, from her Boston experiences, from problems of ill health and the grief of losing loved ones, from inevitable changes in her little community, and even from the recurring cycles in which nature reveals itself mark stages in her development. The final revelation comes to her in the mountains of Colorado on a picnic with her cousins and some friends: "The air was dry and pure, the pines were dark on the steep slopes, the coldness of the water and the turquoise of the sky were beautiful. . . . It was untrue, all the hilarity that was so small and reckless and gay in the midst of this great surrounding beauty. There was something perilous, sorrowful under it" (328).

This experience, of seeing herself in a true perspective, and therefore as small, epitomizes Marjorie's achievement of maturity. She is still unawakened, of course, still virginal. The young man with her on the mountain picnic means nothing to her as a person. But, like Sleeping Beauty, she is ready for the life-giving kiss.

To point to the ordinariness of Marjorie and of the outcome of her quest is not really relevant to the author's achievement.

A marriage is never ordinary to the persons involved, and one of Miss Suckow's firmly held tenets is that all individuals, however undistinguished, are interesting. The author spent two hundred and twenty thousand words to prove that Marjorie Schoessel, a nice little Iowa girl, was a worthy subject for a novel. In doing so, she anticipated Arthur Miller who put the defense of his ordinary hero in the words of Willie's wife—"He has to be paid attention to." Miss Suckow also believed that her Marjorie deserved attention.

In the end we too are ready to accept Marjorie's quest as significant. Though not Homeric, it resembles its original in the part played in it by the forces of Fate. The Olympian gods affect Ulysses' journey; unexpected turns of chance affect Marjorie's. Yet in both cases the protagonist has to keep trying; the hero must be heroic. Marjorie's Odyssey is on a very small scale— perhaps some would call it mock heroic—yet through it all she stubbornly pursues her quest. She is like a slighter, paler country cousin of James's heroine, who, he liked to say, "confronted her destiny." Marjorie was forever governed by her longing to merge her inner desire for truth and beauty with an external life that would feed and support it—that would be, as she stumblingly said, beyond what people called "everyday things."

And there is one more resemblance between the Odysseys. Just as there is no surety that Ulysses will always be happy at home on his quiet island, so it is not certain that Marjorie will never lapse into spoiled discontent on her fruit ranch. Realistically, Miss Suckow has left plenty of leeway for the incertitude of life —her version of the happy ending is very tentative. But the reader is content to leave the heroine there with her hardly won destiny, since he feels what the fates portend is fully right for her.

CHAPTER *4*

Women

THE NOVELS *Country People* and *Odyssey,* as well as the novelettes and early short stories, belong to the first phase of Miss Suckow's career. These early works have in common their poetic quality, derived from the author's desire to capture and make permanent a fleetingly beautiful experience, often through a single character's heightened awareness. The stories are all marked by unity and singleness of purpose; even *Odyssey,* in spite of its great length and multiplicity of incident, can only be understood as a unified quest for self-realization, one so passionately pursued that literally every word contributes to that end.

Miss Suckow's next full-length fictions—*The Bonney Family* (1926), *Cora* (1929), and *The Kramer Girls* (1930)—as well as her occasional short stories, take a new path. Her next three novels—are concerned less with the individual adventures of the soul and more with social relationships: people in their dealings with one another. They can be considered problem novels, the problems having to do with careers, professions, rearing of children, friendships, licit and illicit love affairs, and aspects of the marriage relation. In this kind of novel Miss Suckow's sure hand with details was an invaluable aid in creating that verisimilitude often described as "true to life." She was as skillful as ever in characterization: her people are real human beings, talking and thinking and doing in wholly natural and believable ways. With unfailing honesty she presents the elements of happiness and sadness mixed, and presents outcomes that fall humanly short of the ideal. It is evident that her early desire to perpetuate beauty has broadened to include a sincere search for the truth, truth that often hides elusively beneath the surface, obscured by the complicated interrelationships of everyday existence.

I The Bonney Family

The Bonney Family represents both an expansion of Miss Suckow's powers and a narrowing of her scope. Instead of focusing on one individual, as *Odyssey* does, it presents an entire family. But because the Bonneys are not a typical family, they are of less universal concern; and, while all the Bonney children, except one, are more unusual than Marjorie, for that very reason they are not so representative. In its treatment of the complex interrelationships within the family, the story of the Bonneys foreshadows that of *The Folks*, but it attempts much less; and in its presentation of a group of "interesting" characters it somewhat resembles popular works of the period.

Like Ruth Suckow's own family, the Bonneys are a ministerial household. Fred Bonney, a boyish, warm-hearted man, is loved by his parishioners but not regarded as a great preacher. His wife Myra is a practical soul, daughter of a minister, hence standing in no awe of the church or the ministry. Her outstanding traits are her common-sense wisdom and her calm strength that are equal to the requirements of her four children and her husband's parents who are part of the household.

Warren, the oldest child, is a problem. Highly intelligent, overgrown and awkward, he is shockingly red-haired, and painfully self-conscious about his conspicuous appearance. He tends to draw into himself as an anti-social individualist, but his mother patiently opposes this withdrawal by insisting that he continue to associate with other young people. She firmly believes that time will modify his erratic appearance and that the habit of social intercourse will smooth his rough edges.

The second child, Sarah, matronly for her twelve years, is better adjusted; but she, too, suffers painful moments in her growing up. Friends of her own age are beginning to alter their behavior to attract boys, but Sarah's downrightness will not allow her to follow their example. Besides, she recognizes sorrowfully that she is not a "cute" girl. She is, in fact, a type that recurs in Suckow fictions—in the short story "Strong as a Man," among others—a bluff, hearty personality, physically strong and competent, and with a heart of gold, but lacking feminine graces. Sarah's self-knowledge is the more distressing in that she is excessively maternal, loves babies and all helpless weak creatures, and longs to spend her strength in caring for them. But she is aware that to attain the role of mother, a girl must be "cute"—attractive to the male sex. The younger Bonney daughter, Wilma, fits the requirement more closely, for she adores fashionable clothes—a scarcity in parsonage life—and leaves off her glasses whenever she can to display her prettiness. Her twin, Wilfred, who is more exceptional, loves animals to excess and is as sensitive to his environment—to objects and to places—as his author.

The story of the Bonneys is not exciting, but fairly absorbing. Mrs. Bonney decides they should leave Morning Sun where her husband is, to use a common phrase, "getting into a rut." He has a chance to move to a small city where their denominational headquarters are located and where the children can attend the church college. Mr. Bonney agrees to the move, but his emotional needs are not satisfied in the new job as they have been in his small-town pastorate. Warmly sympathetic by nature, he liked the close relationship with his people as he was called upon to share their deepest experiences.

The other family members, who adjust to the new environment in their own fashion, are sustained by Mrs. Bonney who maintains the home as a comfortable, substantial refuge at the center of their lives. She cares for her husband's parents through their final illnesses, and sees the older children satisfactorily launched. Then she suddenly dies, a few days after an operation that has seemed to be successful. Sarah, called home from settlement work in Chicago, stays on as the bulwark of the family. When the war comes, Wilfred enlists and is lost in France; and Wilma makes an impulsive wartime marriage. Through these crises, Sarah is a sustaining comfort.

The post-war era brings more changes to the family. Wilma and her husband, settled on his parents' farm, are only partially satisfied and happy; and Warren, married to a regulation YWCA type of girl and teaching in a small Montana college, is harassed and frustrated. Sarah is disturbed by his narrow conservatism.

Sarah herself has taken her mother's place at home at the sacrifice of her own ambitions. Her summer at the settlement house has shown her a worthwhile outlet for her strength and capabilities, but she does not grudge giving up this beckoning career. The days and months at home, made peaceful and orderly by her efforts, fill her with a deep satisfaction. Like Marjorie, she loves best of all to be at home when she is needed there. At length, however, change involves her, too. Her father is attracted to a much younger woman, a college professor, whose extravagant vivacity is fed by her desire to lure a man into marriage. Glendora's plight, as she lives a maiden existence with her aging mother and feels life slipping away, is a familiar one to Suckow readers, but only rarely does such a female find a prize like Fred Bonney, sympathetic and warm-hearted, with a boyish innocence about him.

When Sarah sees him rejuvenated by Glendora's flattering attentions, she, with half-rueful understanding, remembers how her mother's calm leadership, as she put it to her brother, "sort of held Dad in" (260). But his other children view the affair in a different light. Wilma deplores his newly acquired spruceness as "obscene in a parent" (262), and Warren rails that his father must be in his dotage, to think of putting "a woman like that in our mother's place" (258). Flouting their disapproval, Sarah faithfully stands by her father through the wedding ceremony, while knowing full well that the preoccupied bridegroom is barely aware of her presence. Then, freed of her responsibility, she makes a short visit to Morning Sun to break old ties, telling friends there that she expects to enter training to become a nurse.

Miss Suckow outlined a sequel to *The Bonney Family* in *Carry-Over*, foretelling Sarah's future. Though her occupation as a welfare worker would expose her to much sorrow and hopelessness, her personal life would be happy and fulfilled. She would eventually marry a widower, a brilliant man but crippled and warped, needing her sane wholesomeness, and she would be able to use her maternal gifts satisfyingly in bringing up his little son.

The Bonney Family is in a certain sense the most readable of Ruth Suckow's works up to this time. Though focused on a minister's family, it devotes no attention to theological problems, except for a passing mention of Sarah's adolescent doubts and questionings. The narrative is centered in the consciousnesses of Mrs. Bonney and Sarah; its concerns are thoroughly domestic; and, since it takes its tone from their characters, it is prevailingly down-to-earth and comfortable. Altogether, it is the kind of book that pleases women readers. And the author's inimitable talent for restoring the actual, caused no less gifted a realist than Sigrid Undset, when introduced to Ruth Suckow's work through this novel, to write enthusiastically to her publisher "I think she writes simply exquisitely.... I am become an ardent admirer of Miss Suckow."[1]

As is usual in Ruth Suckow's fiction, the characters, rather than the incidents, give the book its interest. Mrs. Bonney is the dominating influence in the first half of the narrative; then she is succeeded by Sarah. In a more tightly plotted work this shift would tend to impair unity, but in the episodic plan of *The Bonney Family*, it has no such effect. Similarly, the Bonneys' move from Morning Sun to Frampton does not disrupt the narrative since this is not a study of place but of a family circle. Part of its purpose is achieved in showing Mrs. Bonney's successful re-establishment of a home atmosphere in different and unpromising surroundings. Though home is the central concern, the novel does not focus on marriage. The relations between Fred and Myra Bonney are not probed; they are only lightly touched in the comment made by Sarah at the time of Fred's remarriage. The interrelationship of parents and children is the subject of Miss Suckow's attention.

On the surface, Mrs. Bonney seems to be a notably effectual mother. She takes time to listen to her children's confidences; she is always ready with calm, objective advice. Some of her words of wisdom sound astonishingly like those in the later magazine columns of Eleanor Roosevelt, as when Mrs. Bonney is admonishing Warren, who has been complaining because he must attend a class party with the only other unattached boy, one "Fatty" Granger:

> I think it's absurd to call people by such names as Fatty, anyway. It seems to me very primitive. It's calling attention constantly to something the person would rather have forgotten—perhaps an unimportant thing. You, at least, might call him Roy. You might do him that justice. Probably that fat comes from a wrong diet that might be corrected. Then no one would see anything ridiculous about Roy. He has a good mind. There are men and women much fatter than Roy. But that doesn't keep them from being respected and often brilliant people. (18)

To show how successfully Mrs. Bonney avoids for her children the pitfalls of alienation and neuroses, the author inserts a mirror plot centering around the son of a faculty family at Frampton College. Donald Satterley, a sensitive boy and a gifted pianist, has a mother who lacks the balance to guide him and quarrels bitterly with his father who tries to impose discipline. Donald runs away from home, is brought back, and later suffers a complete physical collapse followed by death. No such fate awaits Warren Bonney, also an exceptional boy; his mother serenely insists on conformity as the means to the good life.

But Sarah sees in Warren an example of a potential for individual greatness that is reduced to mediocrity by this very insistence on acceptable standards. She sees the outcomes of Mrs. Bonney's efforts as less than happy ones, and she says: "Mother worked so hard to help Warren—but it seems as if just because he was so different before, he settled down all the harder. He's just a regular college professor, Mrs. Paulson. You ought to see him. He's the *most* regular kind" (292).

The disunion of the Bonneys at the close of the book—"two dead, and of those who were left, half at enmity with the other half"—is in a way symbolic of the futility of Mrs. Bonney's efforts. Mrs. Paulson, an old family friend, tells Sarah: "I always thought your mother was a great woman. She might have directed some great work if she hadn't had her family. Though that's a foolish way to put it. Not that she 'might have'—she did" (292). This afterthought, however, is not convincing. Sarah's troubled answer reflects the doubt in her author's mind: Would Mrs. Bonney and her children, too, have benefited with less of her managing? But Miss Suckow casts only the shadow of a doubt; in that era, careers outside the home were all but unthinkable for mothers of families.

The yawning abyss between the generations also serves to nullify the efforts of parents to live their children's lives, as Miss Suckow was aware since she had experienced something of the kind herself. Sarah exemplifies this situation in her farewell visit to Morning Sun as she chats companionably with older women, former friends of her mother's. She seems mature, almost of their era. But, when Mrs. Emerson tearfully confides her disappointment in her daughter's marriage (Geraldine Emerson was one of the "cute" girls of Sarah's young days), Sarah is silent. Her sympathies are entirely with Geraldine.

Sarah seems momentarily out of character when she reflects that she was "the least loved, the least cherished of the children" (272). In another place, her feeling is expressed in this way:

"Her own loneliness had both driven her out and set her free" (296). It is obvious that a girl as admirably self-reliant as Sarah would require less coddling and attention than her touchier siblings; therefore, Sarah's plaints have a taint of incongruous self-pity. They are explainable, however, as a rationalization for what always seems a monstrous dereliction in a Suckow heroine— leaving home to strike out for herself. Even though her family no longer needs her, Sarah would feel too guilty in leaving home if she hadn't that excuse: "They didn't love me as well as the rest!"

The Bonney Family owes much to Ruth Suckow's experiences as a minister's daughter. She has a rich store of remembered habits and attitudes to draw on, but for the most part this book is not autobiographical. The family, its situation, and its problems are altogether the product of imagination. Yet this seeking on the part of Sarah to ward off the pangs of self-reproach is attributable to something deep and ineradicable in Miss Suckow's consciousness and is an example, perhaps, of the writer's creativity being fed from underground springs. Miss Suckow draws her most significant insights not from imagination, but from a sort of enlightened perceptiveness.

II Cora

By 1926 Ruth Suckow had established herself as a successful professional writer. She sold her bee farm that year and began spending her winters in New York. Her next two books, *Cora* and *The Kramer Girls*, grew out of new experiences. Though the action of both novels takes place mostly in the familiar Iowa locale, the scene receives only incidental attention. Miss Suckow now turned her observation to matters affecting the new woman, anticipating the feminist dispute which passed through various phases in ensuing years and is still very much with us.

Cora Schweitert, the first of Miss Suckow's modern heroines, is one of the dark girls that, as she confessed in a magazine article entitled "Literary Soubrettes," she had always secretly preferred to the insipid blonde beauties of traditional literature.[2] Cora has all the force and independence needed for the role of rebel, but she turns out not to be a rebel after all. Cora's strength of character spends itself on her family, as, like Jennie, by sheer unflagging effort and self-denial, she hoists the rather ordinary, shiftless lot into a position of substantial respectability. Finding herself adrift with her family in a Midwestern city and in a situation much like that in some of Dreiser's novels, Cora insists that other family members follow her leadership. She is influenced by the example of the people of Warwick, the small Iowa town where the Schweiterts had previously lighted in their wanderings, and where Cora spent a relatively happy interval. Cora reflects on how people in Warwick live, "working, accumulating, sticking to it, gradually building up a slow, solid prosperity" (53).

This reflection of Iowa materialism more than any other element gives the book its Iowa flavor. Cora is like August Kaetterhenry in her firm faith that prosperity will be the outcome of industry and thrift. In her case, as in his, her faith is justified. Her rootless family eventually have a home of their own, with sufficient income from their combined earnings to live comfortably, even pleasantly. In bringing this result about, Cora's hard, ruthless streak allows nothing to interfere with achieving her goals, and she holds a firm rein over her family. She early decrees that her mother is to stay in the home: "There must be some one at home. It couldn't be herself or Sophie—it would have to be mama. It was simply of no use, moving on to another place, as papa wanted to do now. It would be the same thing over again. If papa couldn't make a go of things here, he couldn't anywhere. No. They were to stay. All of them would have to work and finally build up a home for themselves" (51).

Quite naturally, Cora is unsympathetic with her father, the little German tailor who is one of Miss Suckow's happiest creations. Everyone likes Chris Schweitert with his warm-hearted gaiety and love of music, his droll stories made funnier by his comic accent, and his unfailing kindness to children. But, according to Warwick standards (and Cora's), he is a failure. He cannot provide adequately for his sizable family. Cora, who thinks such a man ought not to have married, is her mother's fierce partisan; she resents the life her father subjects them to more on her mother's account than on any other. When he can no longer stand factory work, Chris is reduced to helping his wife cook for boarders and to washing the dishes, about which he makes deprecating little jokes. Finally unable to function even in this capacity, he does small tailoring jobs for people in the neighborhood and talks to the visiting children who adore him. When he dies, Cora exclaims, "Papa seemed to enjoy life more just putter-

ing around than the rest of us did trying to get somewhere!"
(131). Her attitude toward her father resembles August Kaetterhenry's toward his father-in-law—a sort of dispassionate contempt.
Chris is the kind of person with whom practical materialists have
no point of contact, for they frankly regard such a one as useless.

Another character who points up Cora's strong traits is Evelyn
Anderson, her girlhood friend of Warwick days. Evelyn, only
child of a successful businessman and pampered darling of her
parents, is pretty, talented, high-spirited and lovable; she obviously is modeled after Miss Suckow's beloved older sister Ema.
Evelyn and Cora have been inseparable; and, after the Schweitert's removal to Onawa, Evelyn's secure, comfortable life continues to be the lodestar of Cora's strivings. Eventually, the less
fortunate girl can observe with pride that she has been able to
provide herself and her family with a home comparable to the
Anderson's. The difference, of course, is that everything comes
easily to Evelyn; indeed, ease and graciousness are part of her
life. While Cora drudges, everything falls smoothly into Evelyn's
hands—college, success in music, desirable offers of marriage. As
a girl, Evelyn is drawn to Cora's father; the two have in common
their spirit of fun. "Oh I just think your father's lovely" (15),
Evelyn exclaims to Cora on one occasion as the two are leaving
Mr. Schweitert's tailor shop where the younger children love to
play. He has just given away his sample card to the little girls to
be cut up for paper dolls. "Ach, ja," he sighs, "I guess dose
paper doll ladies, dey need some husbands. I send and get me
anudder card" (15).

Cora pursues her business career in the same hard-headed,
shrewd way she manages her family. It is clearly a man's world
she has entered—she is not given the title or distinctions of an
executive position although she bears the responsibilities of one.
Confident, however, that she is indispensable to her employers,
she believes her reward will come. Men she keeps scrupulously
at arm's length, but she accepts their attentions as tributes to her
success and good looks. But this state of affairs changes subtly
after Mr. Schweitert's death and the scattering of the other children into homes of their own. Cora, lonely and bored but still
young and vigorous, longs for the fulfillment as a woman that she
has for so long fiercely denied herself. Just why this longing
should break out so irresistibly at the moment it does is not

satisfactorily explained, but it furnishes the motivation for Cora's setting off on a long-deferred vacation trip through the West.

In Yellowstone Park, during the course of a six-day stage tour, she feels herself drawn as by inexorable fate into romance with Gerald Matthews, a fellow tourist. This section of the novel, devoted to Cora's love affair, is unique. Miss Suckow locates it in scenery far from and strangely different from her usual Iowa background; for that reason, it seems to lack reality. There is a two-dimensional quality about it, with its setting of tall pines, mysterious geysers, high peaks, and waterfalls. The author takes to moving her gaily costumed people around against this backdrop somewhat as she used to manipulate her paper dolls. Because of a stiffness about their movements and their talk, they fail to come alive.

As for Gerald, he is handsome, but he is only a paper man. Cora's need is so great that she leads him on into complete involvement. Too conventional to engage in a transitory affair, she induces him to propose marriage to which she quickly assents. During the short but ecstatic period of Cora's happiness, she blooms ino gorgeousness. The rented apartment in Denver that Gerald provides for them has even a touch of luxury; she relaxes there in unaccustomed ease and devotes time to adorning herself. The passages describing Cora's metamorphosis are well done. The paper doll quality has disappeared, for Ruth Suckow is always convincing when exploring the depths of the feminine consciousness. Gerald is out of the house now, a car salesman making sporadic attempts to sell automobiles. He is in the background, where husbands usually are during these revealing reveries of Suckow heroines, but his presence is deeply felt as the awakening agent, the necessary means for sexual fulfillment. As a beekeeper Miss Suckow was familiar with this pattern. Cora is like a queen bee—Gerald calls her a queen—and Gerald is the lover who must cooperate in her necessary fulfillment and then be discarded. The very name *Cora* means heart, and it is her heart he touches.

It is inevitable that Gerald, after that incredible nuptial flight, should fail to keep up with Cora. He has known from the start that she is his superior; and his excuse-making, weak and deplorable as it is, is due to his devastating knowledge that he cannot live up to her expectations. He finally does the only thing possible—he runs away and leaves his wife alone in a desolate little Colorado town. (The apartment in Denver, rent unpaid, has been abandoned.) He never knows about the baby Cora awaits during despondent months and, alone and bitter in a Denver hospital, finally gives birth to. Cora knows that she could have her husband found and brought back for he still loves her; but she knows even more surely how futile such an action would be. Gerald has sufficed as a lover; he cannot cope as a husband and father.

The final section of *Cora* brings her, sadly disillusioned, back to her home in Onawa. There, with her aging mother and Aunt Soph to look after little Josephine, Cora eventually resumes her business career and the support of her household. Though her marriage has been a disastrous one, she comes to recognize it as somehow fated—as a snatching at the delight she glimpsed with Evelyn in their Warwick girlhood. It has brought her grief and pain but a deeply felt joy, too, that she cannot bring herself to wish she had never experienced. As for Evelyn, who trusted and gave herself to life with such unbounded eagerness, embracing it all—her music, her young husband, her babies, her brilliant social existence—she has met an early death.

"They had come to the same thing," Cora reflects, "her own bitter struggle through pain and necessity, and Evelyn's eager and trustful security" (306). And later, musing in the company of her latest admirer, who is rich, elderly, and unhappily married, Cora thought that "People really did get what they were after—only in such queer, unrealized ways, changed and unrecognizable, and, perhaps, at the price of everything else. She did not know that she would really change what she had" (332).

The resemblance of *Cora* to some of Dreiser's novels has been remarked—the Naturalist treatment of the Schweiterts' sordid circumstances after their move to the city, with Cora peeling potatoes in the cold, disordered kitchen and resolving fiercely that her mother shall no longer go out to work; and the pessimistic view of things that Cora adopts after her disastrous marriage, tinged by the fatalism that "made her feel her smallness in the huge and almost incomprehensible midst of existence" (305). But Miss Suckow is only fleetingly like Dreiser. Being a woman, she realizes Cora and her other women characters with greater subtlety than Dreiser is capable of doing with his *Jennie* and

Carrie. And, though both writers glimpse the "eternal tragedy of man," to repeat Mencken's phrase, her view is predominantly human rather than cosmic, as Dreiser's is, and more specifically leveled at the pains and problems of the female sex.

Probably because *Cora* is the result of some rather hard thinking on the subject of feminism, it is the toughest-fibered of Ruth Suckow's novels. The poetic quality of the early short stories is almost completely lacking, as is the tender, nostalgic treatment of well-loved things and places. Because of her immersion in practical concerns, Cora has developed little appreciation for spiritual values; her author is somewhat out of her element in dealing with such a character. She reproduces Cora's thoughts with difficulty; some of the interior monologue is strained and obscure. Cora is a real and convincing person, however, and serves well to make her author's points. From her story we are apprised of Miss Suckow's conviction that women are fully competent to succeed in a man's world, even if they are often expected to do twice the work of their masculine counterparts. There are many instances in which women are clearly men's superiors. Marriage often means that a woman must repress her own abilities to fit the scope of her mate and to keep him flattered and content.

But Miss Suckow does not belabor the unfairness of men to women or even the inequity of the system. The predominant theme in *Cora* and in other works is that women have chiefly themselves to combat. Basic in every woman, even the most mannish or the hardest or most ruthless of the sex, is her desire to yield. Cora's unhappiness is due to her discovery that her impulsive and ill-considered marriage has joined her to a man to whom it is impossible for her to continue to yield. The very traits that Cora's life was built on—industry, thrift, and orderly integrity—are those he utterly lacks.

By creating a character with the shortcomings of Gerald Matthews, the author has made further argument impossible. Feminist or non-feminist, nobody could ask Cora to make the best of her marriage with Gerald. Cora herself considers it at times: "She was thinking of how it might have been if she had actually looked for Gerald, sought him out, given her strength to his weakness, yielded all the purpose of her life to him, and, through all the pain and failure, kept the softness of her love" (332).

But Gerald is too completely untrustworthy. What would have happened, one might rather ask, if he had been only slightly weak, not quite Cora's equal, or a failure as a breadwinner, as her father had been? To explore that situation would need another set of characters, another novel; and this work Miss Suckow, still pondering the situation of women in today's world, resolved to write.

III   The Kramer Girls

As the title indicates, *The Kramer Girls* is not a study of one individual but of a family of sisters. Family life was of great concern to Miss Suckow, as all her previous works indicated; in the Kramer family she shows it under unusual and difficult circumstances. The mother of the Kramer girls is a hopeless paralytic; and Rose, the youngest child, has been cared for since babyhood by Georgie and Annie, her much older sisters, who also run the household and care for their mother. The father, a shadowy figure, is a tight-fisted curmudgeon held vaguely responsible for the mother's ill health.

Both her older sisters are absurdly proud of Rose's wholesome good looks and scholastic excellence, but it is Georgie who insists that she "make something of herself." Georgie is strong and capable; and, had things been different—if her mother's health had not tied her down and if educational opportunities had been forthcoming—she would have excelled in a career of her own. Personally thwarted, she transfers her ambitions to Rose. Georgie wheedles and maneuvers the money for Rose's college expenses from their father, sure that with Rose's own demonstrated ability, the younger sister will be able to do what Georgie has not been able to. It seems to Rose that "Georgie had put a great destiny upon her" (40).

Rose, docile and amenable to Georgie's plans for her, even gives up her budding romance with Hammie, who plays basketball and is irresistibly charming, though, as Georgie points out, "no good." She goes on to college and makes Phi Beta Kappa. There her best friend is Jane, a strong-minded girl bent on being an actress. Later Georgie helps Rose borrow the money to go to Chicago with Jane and launch herself in a business career while Jane tries the theater. When Rose is called back home after a year in the city because of her mother's imminent death, Georgie laments that Rose is detained from her fascinating job and big-time excitements while her mother lingers.

But the truth emerges that Rose does not feel as Georgie would feel. Rose is not Georgie, but Rose; and she is rather guiltily glad to be at home. An affectionate girl, she loves all the landmarks of her home; indeed, she is as moved by the magic of place as her author. As she washes dishes in the familiar kitchen,

> Rose felt that something had to happen to get her away from her job—from all jobs, from being lost in the hard stony world of business and crowded city streets and mechanical devices and cramped, impersonal living quarters, that she knew were alien. . . . Whenever she looked out of the window, she could see—above the muslin sash curtain—her own little plum tree, that she loved as no other, because it seemed to have shared in all the personal happiness and unhappiness of her life. Sunshine poured in through the window and glinted off the clean wet dishes; and Rose felt as if she were bathing in this sunshine . . . and in open-ness, peace, personal affections, continuity—all these were in the sensuous blessing of the sunshine. (122)

Two things happen to keep Rose happily at home: Jane suddenly leaves for New York, disrupting their Chicago venture; and Rose encounters Archie Carpenter, a pleasant young man in the building trade, whom she has known slightly in school days. "Archie represented all that was best and dearest to her in the old life, the life of home" (148), and her response to him is natural and immediate. Not daring to tell Georgie, who, she knows, will disapprove, Rose marries Archie secretly even before her mother's death. Although Rose's marriage does not please Georgie, the older woman soon has other things to occupy her. Georgie and Annie, freed by their mother's death and by their father's subsequent remarriage, move to "the Rapids," a bustling small city, and there find congenial work; Annie, as a clerk in a department store; Georgie, as a chiropractor. By a queer reversal of fate, they become career girls and Rose becomes the stay-at-home.

A new and different existence is opened to Rose by her marriage. For the first time, she feels that her life is really her own (except that she has given it to Archie). In the spring sunshine, planting seeds in the garden of the raw little house Archie had built to sell,

She was humming—the secretly exultant hum of inward concentration and outward abstraction: the kind that bees make when the honey flow is just past the first excited beginnings, when fields of flowers lie before them almost stealthy in their fragrance, but the heat and heavy work of the harvest is not yet upon them. . . .

So the lovely day passed with a sort of ritual, from event to event. The spring sunshine brightened it all. The household happiness grew, deepened, and expanded. (161)

After a time, her happiness is tempered by the realization that Archie is not very enterprising—a good workman, but one contented to work for others. When Georgie visits, she shrewdly observes that the little household, now including two children, is in reduced circumstances. Although Rose responds to the hearty, sympathetic comfort of her prosperous older sister, she appreciates Archie's goodness—and the goodness and simplicity of Archie's mother, who opens her home to them in Archie's slack times. The same mystic rhythm that Rose felt in the early days of her marriage regulates the older woman's existence and draws the two together. Rose reflects: "Within those tiny limits how wisely, how satisfactorily, how thoroughly she lived! Rose loved Archie's mother . . ." (185).

But life is less simple for Rose than for Archie's mother. It is complicated for the younger woman by her education, by Georgie's plans for her, and by what people expect of her. She shrinks from meeting old friends on the street, aware that they know that Archie has had to bring his family home to his mother's. Her clothes are shabby, and she also wants more advantages for the children. In fact, Rose is pulled in two directions. Employable as she is, she knows she can solve part of her difficulties by going to work, but she really does not want to do so. It would be an open admission of Archie's inadequacy; it would hurt Archie; but more to the point, it would also hurt Rose. As Miss Suckow puts it: "Rose wanted (with a sense of aching defraudment) him to come up to herself. She had tried to narrow herself and to deny her own capability. Now it hurt and angered her that she could not" (231). Like all Suckow heroines, Rose longs for the deep satisfaction of submitting herself to a mate she regards as stronger and more able than herself. This intrinsic feminine quality would be violated if she took over part of the support of the family. She wants Archie to protest—to try to prevent her; but he will not.

Georgie watches the Carpenters' struggles from the point of view of one who has always regarded Archie as "a weak sister," to use her Iowa vernacular. At one point she tells herself ruefully that "she might as well have let Rose have her fun with Hammie in the first place." But Georgie herself, with all her strength and self-confidence, is also forced to learn some hard lessons. She has established herself in an occupation she likes and does well at; the future looks bright; and then suddenly, incredibly, cancer strikes her. During the long period in the hospital, Georgie has time to think deeply. She tells her sister Annie, "It'll be better for the kid [Rose] to have me gone. She won't have me, and then she'll have to stand on her own feet. . . . Folks can't do much for other folks" (219).

Georgie's conclusion matches that of Sarah Bonney's about her mother: managing other people's lives is a questionable course. This truth is only one of the many embedded in the story of the Kramer sisters. They are studies in feminism, exemplifying three types of women—the two extremes and the mean between them. Georgie is the mannish type, probably meant to remain single, though even she owns a secret admiration for a rich and cultivated fellow townsman, who though given to remarking, "Georgie Kramer is a fine woman," at the same time bestows his warmest glances on the blooming Rose. Then, too, some of Georgie's fierce independence—her declaration, for example, that women ought not to have to rely on marriage as their only way of earning a living—may be attributable to the gloominess of her home situation. But indications are that Georgie could succeed as a career woman if anyone could. The largeness of her scope allows her to substitute service to humanity for the more circumscribed duties to husband and family. Her death at the height of her usefulness is a tragic waste— another justification for the writer's frequent protest against the unfairness of "things as they are."

Annie, who receives less attention, is an example of the universal feminine. Sweet, domestic, and thoroughly conforming, she has been passed over by admirers because her home responsibilities have made her less available than other girls. By the time she is free, she has settled into gentle spinsterhood, lavishing affection on her cat, watching avidly the affairs of the high school set, and gossiping with other maiden ladies. Rose senses in Annie that "feminine grossness" that Miss Suckow often notes—it is spoken of as something "ancient" and is probably to be understood as elemental in the female sex. It reveals itself in an excess of interest in the functions of women: household matters, of course, but more specifically those having to do with the female body, its peculiar ailments, sexual maladjustments, and details of births and operations. Annie's job in the piece goods department in Hofthaler's Store is suitably domestic. There is even a male functionary in charge for "the girls" to twitter over and please. After Rose establishes herself as a secretary, she recognizes this tendency for unmarried women in business to identify with their employers in a quasi-married relationship; she is thankful that her own happy marriage has saved her from this weakness.

For Rose is feminine, just as Annie is. Tenderness is her chief quality. At first Georgie is able to prevent its natural outcome in the affair with Hammie. The following passage indicates how deep-seated is her desire to yield:

> Rose used to have a kind of day-dream that always frightened her. She would think, "What if I were up in a tree and let go of the branches?"—and she would feel herself falling. . . .The sensation was terrifying, dizzy and yet strangely sweet. Now she had that same old sensation again. She was sunk, unstirring, in the incredible happiness of Hammie's embrace. The snow fell all about them, soothed them, shut them in. But again, in the bottom of her heart, it seemed to her a dark, mute, frightened pain growing. She didn't consciously think of Georgie, but a burden of guilt was upon her. . . . (29-30)

Though Rose achieves the destiny as wife and mother for which she is so clearly meant, she is not allowed an untroubled acceptance. And Georgie's tampering—her inflicting of her own philosophy and ambitions on the younger, impressionable girl— is not the only stumbling block. Modern conditions also serve to complicate her life. Miss Suckow was well aware that girls were being trained for careers and that the working woman was here to stay. She was aware, too, of the strains and stresses marriage must suffer as a result. It is typical of her that she is most deeply concerned with the subtle threat to the personal lives of the marriage partners.

The solution of Rose's problem is a compromise. Her affectionate nature and her strong sense of continuity will save her marriage, together with the fact that, despite her high scholastic standing in school and in college, she is quite an ordinary female after all. Her friend Jane, on the other hand, like Marjorie's Emily in *Odyssey,* is an example of a more fully emancipated woman. Jane finds it possible to tear herself from the restraining bonds of family and to defy conventions in her personal life. Rose is not so exceptional. Her home is described as comfortable but "commonplace," and so is she. Though she will never be a brilliant success as an independent woman, she is capable enough to handle both home duties and her office position competently— something accepted today but which Rose's prospective employer questions. "As a rule, we're not inclined to employ married women in this office," he tells her. "You feel sure you can handle the home question and the office, too?" (238).

Besides being essentially feminine, Rose Kramer is notable for her sensitive response to nature, the changing seasons, and the movement through all its different phases that marks the progress of each day. She senses, as Thoreau did, the riches to be garnered from this awareness, but she has not Thoreau's genius which permitted him to deviate from the ways of "the masses of men." Both her limited endowments and her environmental conditioning unfit her, for example, for accepting the kind of life her mother-in-law lived, idyllically satisfying as she finds that life to be in some of its aspects.

This attunement of Rose is beautifully conveyed in the most poetic passages in the book. Miss Suckow has endowed it with special significance. She seems to suggest that this response of a loving and natural woman to primal things, to the pulse of life itself, is not merely an idiosyncrasy but a birthright held in common by all women. That it is rejected or neglected in most cases and allowed to dissipate itself in artificial diversions is the author's serious charge against the conditions of modern society.

IV   Children and Older People

Children and Older People, published in 1931, is a collection of Miss Suckow's short stories that appeared in *American Mercury, Good Housekeeping,* and *Harper's* in the years following 1925. Several of these, reminiscent of the author's childhood, are doubtless by-products of her dredging among her memories during the writing of *Odyssey.* One or two about old people resemble those in *Iowa Interiors.* But most of them appeared during the period of *The Bonney Family, Cora,* and *The Kramer Girls;* and they reflect the same shift in emphasis from the beauty of experience to practical problems of living. The stories are, in general, more prosaic than the early ones; yet because of the demands of the form, its compression and brevity, they still bear resemblance to the lyric poem and are marked by that poetic quality that is the hallmark of Ruth Suckow's best writing. At this point, short stories, her kind of short stories, still seemed to be a more natural outlet for her particular talent than the novel.

The content of many of these stories reflects a growing concern with the complications a woman meets in the relationships of love and marriage. Miss Suckow, always a partisan of and spokesman for her sex, seems to feel that many women, bound by inarticulateness and convention, are unable to speak for themselves. As a woman herself, in her thirties and still unmarried, she evinces a curiosity about the effect of marriage on the feminine personality. All these stories, except those specifically about children, treat of some aspect of marriage or love affairs, though with wide variance. They present honest and valid observations, but in every case observations only. They are studies of marriage by an outsider, observing closely and thinking deeply—but still an outsider. But this statement does not apply, however, to the incidents from childhood included in this collection. These draw their vitality from their actuality; here is again that exquisitely right choice of detail: the evocation of feeling about persons, places, and things that made *Odyssey* such a living experience and the members of the Bonney family so touchingly true to life.

"Eminence," one of these re-creations of reality, is about an oldtime Christmas program in a small-town church; and it carries its readers back to Iowa in the early 1900's. There is quiet irony in the title: the star of the program is little five-year-old Florentine Watkins, cast as the Christmas fairy. Yet the magnitude of the occasion, at that time and in that place, leaves no doubt that Florentine, wearing her star-studded crown, is truly eminent. The excitement of Christmas Eve, the sparkling winter night, the lights on the Christmas tree—all give Florentine the rating of a star.

The author uses a flexible point of view, moving it about like a spotlight. First it points up the Watkins parents, tense and preoccupied, over-eager to show off their child, and communicating their tension to the little girl; then the parents of more ordinary children; then the program, as it progresses through run-of-the-mill numbers. It finally focuses on the consciousness of Florentine while she waits her turn, her heart beating painfully as she feels the overwhelming compulsion of every prima donna to distinguish herself. She rises to the occasion; her part is a success; and the applause is warm. After the peak of her achievement, everything is anticlimactic to Florentine. Her parents have brought her Christmas present, a huge, fantastically expensive doll, to be presented by Santa Claus with the rest of the gifts at the close of the exercises. This gift is felt by the other parents to be an over-ostentatious one. The children, sensing Florentine's superiority, shut her out as they play companionably about the church before going home. In a small way, Florentine is the victim of the alienation her eminence has imposed upon her. The end of the evening finds her tired and disspirited.

In spite of the juvenility of its leading character, the implications of this little narrative move it beyond the limits of a children's story. The setting apart of the gifted child (even her over-decorative name "Florentine" contrasts with those of her little friends Lola and Lucy) suggests injudicious parental handling as well as the inevitable loneliness of the artist. Ruth Suckow, an accomplished "speaker of pieces" in her early youth, and subject as well to the attention centered on the minister's family, probably knew many moments of lonely isolation like Florentine's. The story leaves us with an uneasy question: Aren't ordinary people happier after all?

"A Little Girl from Town" is about another over-indulged and over-sheltered child—a little princess, like the one in "Four Generations." The point of this story is not Patricia's alienation but the contrast between her way of life as a town child and that of the country children she is briefly visiting. These children belong to a large family, a relatively poor and uncultivated one. They cluster around the little city miss, admiring her delicacy, her exquisite clothes, her air of being from a different world. Unconsciously, however, they reveal advantages their life possesses. The maternal sweetness of the oldest farm child, Leone, as she accepts the responsibility of caring for the little visitor, at the same time keeping peace within her own brood (she reminds us of Jennie in *The Best of the Lot*), betrays the warmth of their family relationship. They are eager to show Patricia their possessions and to entertain her by a visit to the barn where newborn kittens are hidden. There is a naturalness in their association with animals and growing things.

The climax of the visit occurs when its purpose is revealed. Patricia's Uncle Dave, gathering up Patricia to take her home, also prepares to take one of the farmer's calves into town to be butchered for veal. The little city girl's violent distress and opposition betray her ignorance of the exigencies of life that are accepted matter-of-factly by the country children. The farmer and his wife are uncomfortable and embarrased. Uncle Dave leaves the calf behind for the farmer to deliver later. The final scene, in which the man and the doomed calf gaze into each other's eyes in puzzlement, brings to mind Miss Suckow's frequent utterance: "Why do things have to be as they are?"

"The Valentine Box" is a slight incident from childhood told as a bedtime story by a mother to her little daughter. Seemingly simple because of its strictly limited point of view, it, too, opens vistas of thought to the adult reader. Robert Frost, in a letter of praise to Ruth Suckow on the publication of *Children and Older People*, which he called her "big little book," singled out this tale for special comment, saying: "How you can write and remember. Your story about the little girl who sent herself Valentines almost makes me want to tell one about a little boy who went to a birthday party he hadn't been invited to. Talk about anguish."[3]

In relating the particulars of that sad Valentine's Day, the mother's half-rueful tone and pregnant pauses speak eloquently through her simple words. The reader learns that she experienced a bitter introduction to the cruelty of childhood, a cruelty not very different from that of the adult world. Among the little girls of this strange town where she has come to live round wool caps, not kitty hoods, are the badges of membership of the in-group. And valentines are status symbols awarded to those whose popularity is an accepted fact. The unspoken distress of the dislocated child bespeaks the author's personal knowledge of painful moves from one small town to another.

"Big Kids and Little Kids," while centered in the consciousness of a little girl and her passionate longing to follow her older sister into the half-sensed delights of adolescents' games, involves as well the parents' pangs at their first-born's approaching womanhood. The end-of-summer weather and the hint of fall in the air induce something like abandon in the older children as they engage in the last wild games of the season and of their childhood. As the little girl is stirred to frenzy by what she cannot fully understand, the games take on a ritual significance and imbue the story with sadness approaching desperation which often accompanies the recognition of inevitable change.

A companion piece to "A Start in Life," "The Man of the Family" portrays a widow's oldest child who is starting out to earn. The obvious difference is that Gerald is a boy and can assert himself. Daisy has been admonished by her mother to work hard so that she will be asked to stay on in her job, but Gerald does his own asking, in a downright aggressive way. Complexity is added to this story in the character of Art Fox, a widower who is beginning to pay attention to Gerald's mother. A mixture of juvenile jealousy, protectiveness and loyalty to his dead father is apparent in Gerald as he sits brooding on the steps after repulsing Art Fox. His mother is also beset by a conflict of emotions: Her normal feminine desire to be loved and cherished by a mate is overcome by her mother love for the little boy who resembles and emulates his father. Miss Suckow's characteristic view of masculine responsibility and feminine sacrifice, to be explored later in *The Folks*, is briefly projected here.

Older people are represented in the collection in two character studies, "Spinster and Cat" and "Midwestern Primitive." The first chronicles a day in the life of Toldine, an elderly German woman who is unmarried and alone except for her cat. Next door, Toldine's sister Henrietta lives with her son and his noisy family. But Toldine is not lonely; she is one of those who know how to live. And Sammy is "company," for the spinster and cat are very close. Orderliness and economy are mainstays in the life of both. For them the day has a ritual order—it is compartmentalized, each part designed for its appropriate tasks. These rites, performed with deliberateness and grace, are as full of meaning as

the gestures in a worship ceremony—Toldine is the priestess;
Sammie, the acolyte:

> Toldine and Sammie were ready for the real business of the day.
> . . . She went about looking at plants with minute attention. She
> picked the withered pinks and threw them upon the little heap
> of plant debris she was piling up at the edge of the garden. She
> tied twine around the spreading phlox. She found out just where
> the dry earth needed digging with her gritty little trowel about
> the flower roots. She filled two wooden buckets (candy buckets,
> the store man had given them to her, they had cost nothing),
> and then to and from these she made excursions with an old tea
> pot and put just the amount of water needed upon just the plants
> that must have it. . . . Sammie followed her about for a while
> through the garden in the fresh morning sunshine. Certain mat-
> ters called for his attention, and others for hers. There was a
> patch of warm earth where he must roll. It was necessary for
> him to keep an eye on a gopher entrance. He was on the look-
> out for birds, too, although this Toldine would never admit to
> Henrietta. They praised him for bringing mice and then scolded
> him for catching birds! "How are you to know?" Toldine de-
> manded in cajoling indignation. (261)

Not only does Toldine understand Sammie—she is cat-like herself. She is slyly "snooping" as she stands on a box in the wood-
shed to spy on John Carpenter, her philandering neighbor on the
other side. But she says nothing: "She lets folks go their way."
And she says of Sammie: "If she didn't interfere with their way,
why should she interfere with his? After all, Sammie was a cat.
He would have to take his chances and live his own way. She
didn't blame him" (274). Toldine's philosophy reflects Miss
Suckow's characteristic sympathy with the individual's assertion
of selfhood; and, as a matter of course, she extends this sympathy
to the lower animals. One's kind of life is plainly determined by
the individual's own qualities. Toldine, so set in her ways, is
tolerant after all.

"Midwestern Primitive" features another individualist—Bert
Statzer's German mother. Bert's efforts to make her small-town
home into a modern tea room and to serve meals prepared according to recipes in women's magazines from tables adorned
with paper decorations are thwarted by her mother's interference. Bert is a tense, over-eager hostess. But the old woman is

incorrigible. Relaxed and comfortable in old clothes and flat-heeled shoes, she waddles smilingly in upon "the company." A natural scene stealer, she knows just how to play up her foreign differences. She displays her charming old country garden, and serves homemade dandelion wine. The guests, unimpressed by Bert's attempts to be citified, are delighted with the primitiveness of Mrs. Hohenschu. Ironically, though Bert does not suspect this, they have patronized her out-of-the-way place in the hope of finding just such old-fashioned simplicity as she scorns and her mother offers.

Miss Suckow reveals her preoccupation with the feminine psyche in portraying a mannish spinster whom her friends refer to as "a great Mollie." (The story first appeared in *Harper's* under the title "Strong as a Man.") Mollie likes to drive around the country in a second-hand Ford, ostensibly taking orders for undergarments, but really reveling in adventures along the road —picking up tramps, lending a hand with stalled cars and run-away farm animals, much in the manner of a boy escaping from school. Mollie is one of the bluff, hearty types that seem to fascinate Miss Suckow, possibly because she was herself so very different. Mollie is loud-voiced, crude, and vital. She has no dread of dirt and motor grease. She associates with men on a footing of equal give-and-take. But she is more kindhearted and generous than any of her friends (too generous for her own good, they say); and in the depths of her dark eyes there is a secret glow of tenderness that gives her away. "She is a woman after all," her crony Frank tells himself, "and therefore unaccountable" (217). The author deliberately makes Mollie as mannish as possible in order to show that all women have that quality of femininity at the very heart of their being. Frank's wife knows that Mollie will not go to Chicago on a fortune-hunting adventure and leave her family—that core of tenderness will not let her abandon those who have a claim on her and might need her ministerings. Women in Miss Suckow's world do not leave home readily. Marjorie's long Odyssey is necessary to bring her to that point; Sarah Bonney, even when no longer needed, feels pangs of guilt when striking out on her own. Women's place is in the home.

"Experience," which shows the emotional shock suffered by a young girl whose brief, intense love affair has ended in the sudden death of her beloved, has even less incident than the other stories. Elizabeth mopes about her quiet home, inconsolable, resisting her parents' efforts to bring her back into the normal flow of daily happenings. She treasures the poignancy of her pain, realizing that it is all she has left of her experience and that its fading will leave her nothing; she is learning the lesson that not to feel is to die.

The attempt in "Experience" is beyond anything Miss Suckow has tried before, for she has given the story cosmic overtones. She manages to catch something of Elizabeth's sharpened vision of the mortality all around her—the flowers on the lawn that must inevitably fade, her parents gently growing older in contrast with the innocent youthfulness of their wedding photograph, even the houses of the little town and the life in them ever changing. All this is delicately balanced against her remembered joy at the height of her love when she felt herself "part of the whole blossoming world" (136). Her expression of her grief is purposely understated as she says stumblingly to Miss Gurney: "When things happen to people, how can they stand to go on living? Why don't they simply die?" (144). Elizabeth is mortally wounded, but she cannot die. She "seemed to feel, at a far distance, her own suffering sinking slowly into the darkness of trees and ground that had held everything before it" (145).

Susan in "Susan and the Doctor" is another young woman who suffers loss, but not through death. Susan's affair with the doctor is an illicit one—he is prevented from marrying because of the women in his family, a demented old aunt and an invalid mother. Susan, a gay, independent business girl, popular with men from her early teens, finds herself really in love for the first time as she responds to the doctor's need of her. She subdues her natural joyousness to suit the secret nature of their association, and, as time goes on, develops a tenderness and compassion that she feels are "beyond her nature." But when the doctor's mother dies and the town expects the couple to marry, he prefers to break with Susan and to begin a courtship leading to marriage with a more exciting, younger girl.

Susan's situation, by no means unusual, is given import through the author's sympathetic understanding of her woman's nature and the sensitive portrayal, against the background of Iowa weather and seasons, of her emotional states. Very touching is

Susan's awareness of the unfair demands made upon her at the final parting—demands significant of the relationship throughout its long course. The doctor insists that she assure him she feels as he does and "understands." "They had both had the best out of this, hadn't they? What was the use of dragging it on? And he had never, in his whole life, felt a moment of freedom to be himself . . ." (43). He can not even leave her without her reassurance; she can not help giving it. Sacrifice is the usual lot of Miss Suckow's women characters.

That marriage does not always bring happiness, moreover, is suggested by the story of Mrs. Kemper who seemingly has everything—a well-to-do husband, pleasant home, two fine grown-up sons. She is accepted into the best society in town; for, besides occupying a substantial position as Mrs. Kemper, she is herself a lady, though somewhat humble and unsure in her stance. Her uncertainty is born of the knowledge that her husband married her after he had deeply loved and lost in death a former sweetheart. He turned to the woman now his wife as second choice while still grief-stricken; and though their life together has been placid and his treatment of her irreproachable, he has never once told her he loved her. She feels therefore that she has no right to accept with joy what should be hers as a wife and mother. The portrait of Mrs. Kemper is convincingly drawn—possibly from some shrinking, sad-eyed prototype observed by Miss Suckow. But the explanation of her problem seems hardly plausible—a hypothesis suggested to the mind of an unmarried and imaginative outsider.

"Good Pals" presents a more usual complication—that of young parents whose closeness to each other is threatened by their responsibilities to their children. Here, as usual, the woman's problem is examined. Hazel is the epitome of the conscientious, perhaps over-conscientious, parent; but she also longs to be a companion to her husband. On a mountain vacation in Colorado, Hazel and Ray plan a moonlight excursion to a high peak to watch the sunrise together; the children are to be left behind. When one of the boys becomes ill and frightened, and they are called back to Halfway Cabin, Ray mutters bitterly: "It's no use trying to do anything when you have kids" (68). After some heated interchanges, they give up the moonlight jaunt. Hazel recognizes the Halfway Cabin as her fate—"halfway mother, halfway wife, halfway person" (70). Compromise is the essence of her life, and sacrifice, too; for their ideal since their college courtship days has been to watch the sunrise together from a mountain peak.

In "Good Pals," the obstacle in the Benson's marriage is the children; in "Charlotte's Marriage," it is the wife's parents. Charlotte and Ken also were college lovers; "a wonderful couple," Ken was a campus leader, and Charlotte an "ideal" girl. Her parents are substantial business people who expect their daughter's husband to "take hold" in the job they arrange for him and to "make good" in order to provide her with accustomed comforts and luxuries. But Ken, it turns out, has no business brains and is a disappointment to his father-in-law. When the older man undertakes to run the younger one's life, trouble develops; and Charlotte is forced to choose between her husband and her parents. The result is the young couple's escape to California, where Charlotte is later discovered by a girlhood friend, living in semi-poverty, lonely for home and parents, but steadfastly loyal to her husband.

There are other complications in this story that is told from the point of view of Grace, the old friend. Grace has remained in Iowa, has married a successful man, and is treating herself to some fun on a winter vacation alone in California. Her long-time envy of Charlotte, of her personality, *joie de vivre*, and romantically ideal marriage, has led her to search out her old friend and discover her circumstances. Though she finds Charlotte faded and her house undistinguished, the envy persists; it is sharpened anew by Charlotte's revealed role as a sympathetic counselor and a vital center of her home.

CHAPTER 5

Folks

THE END of the 1920's marked the end of an era for Ruth Suckow. During that marvelous decade she had established a successful business which had sustained her during the launching of her writing career, and she had produced five novels and some thirty short stories and articles that placed her among the leaders of a brilliant literary movement. During the latter part of this period, while living in New York, she saw much of another young Iowan, Ferner Nuhn, who had read all her work and who had sought her out when she was living in Earlville, driving over, as he says, "from his own family home in Cedar Falls in a Ford."[1]

Mr. Nuhn had also won Mencken's attention and had had short stories published in the *Mercury*. In New York as a free lance writer he did a number of book reviews including one of *The Bonney Family* which was remarkable not only for its taste and sensitiveness, but for the profound appreciation it conveyed of the author's individual gifts and what she was trying to do with them. The friendship of the two writers deepened, and in the spring of 1929 they were married in San Diego.

Their marriage welded their two careers and had an immense significance in both their lives. For some fifteen years they lived in various places about the country—in New York for a time, then in New England, some of the time at writers' and artists' colonies. Miss Suckow's long novel *The Folks* was begun during these years and was completed in Washington, D.C., while her husband was serving as a specialist in information for the United States Department of Agriculture under Henry Wallace. Published in 1934, the novel was named by the Literary Guild as its October book choice.

I *Genesis of* The Folks

In *The Folks* Ruth Suckow's artistic development reached its culmination. The tentative, youthful quality evident in some of her early work is entirely missing from this book. It is clear that the author has found herself. Her accomplished success, her maturity (she reached her fortieth year during the writing of *The Folks*) and her marriage brought her an assured authority. There is a relaxed sense of power evidenced in the successive portions of this work, as if the writer flexed her well-practiced muscles with the delight of a skilled craftsman.

The novel gives a sense of finality, too, gathering themes from previous works and combining them in a conclusive utterance. Like *Country People, The Folks* is a portrayal of a culture; like *Odyssey,* it is concerned with the quest of individuals for self-fulfillment; and like *The Bonney Family,* it is the chronicle of a family, complicated by the relationships among its various members. Feminism, the chief concern of *Cora* and *The Kramer Girls,* is an important theme in *The Folks;* and the treatment of marriage, noted in a number of the earlier short stories, is continued in the extensive probing of that subject in this novel.

From the time of her early lyric utterances about lives she observed, Miss Suckow devoted much thought to her Iowans, occasionally summing up these musings in provocative articles on the subject. In one of these, entitled "Iowa" and published in *American Mercury* (September, 1926), she classified the levels of culture in the state. Aware of the materialistic purpose which had underlain Iowa's settlement and development, she called its attitude toward culture "timid and fidgety" (39). The men, busy with getting ahead, left all cultural concerns to women's clubs, to the ministers and to the denominational colleges of the area. The New England element in the population was respected as culturally superior; there were always a few old ladies who brought to mind the Concord group of learned sages. Between this exalted segment and the earthy base of working farmers there were a number of other gradations. In the towns there was an echo of Babbitry, though Iowans as she saw them were too humble to boast blatantly; below this prosperous civic group was a bitter, barren Main Street segment; below it, the retired farmers, grim and tight-fisted, lived on their incomes from active years on the farm and were utterly without intellectual and cultural interests. At the base were the working farmers, whom Ruth Suckow regarded as the foundation of Iowa life; she found them plain, fresh, substantial, and unpretentious—she celebrated their characteristics in *Country People.* In *The Folks* she proposed to include the other elements, represented by the people of the small towns.

Toward the end of the decade that marked her arrival as an important literary force, Miss Suckow spoke out again regarding literature and the arts in the Midwest. She had observed the exodus from the region of young intellectuals, who were loud in their denunciations that their home towns were "dead" and had nothing with which to nourish the creative spirit. These "arty" young people sought folk expression in Europe and in out-of-the-way sections of this country—in the American Southwest, in the Southern Appalachians, in Pennsylvania Dutch settlements. In a challenging article, "The Folk Idea in American Life,"[2] Miss Suckow insisted that the Midwest possessed a rich abundance of folk materials; but she explained that, because of the region's rapid rise to affluence, these folk qualities tended to be buried under a prosperous modern exterior that was too standardized to be interesting to the culture-hunter. She pointed out that the Midwest had been settled by bands of people with a common purpose—to achieve prosperity—and that the communities reflected both this purpose and the communal nature of their quest. The early settlements were like a big family; they were "the folks" rather than the folk. The family was the important unit, often referred to as "the folks"; the term "folks" was applied as well to members of the community at large.

With her usual perceptiveness, Miss Suckow analyzed the early culture of pioneer Iowa that had been dependent on the predominating establishments, the church and the school. She recalled that spelling bees and literary evenings were held at the school; quilting bees and Sunday School programs were common to the church. When rapid prosperity brought modern living to the region within the time span of one generation, the culture patterns remained under a new guise. The institutions of the earlier days, the church and the school, were still the centers of the town's entertainment, but they now offered lectures, class plays, and athletic contests that were enjoyed by the whole community. The writer's deep appreciation of the "folks" and their qualities inspired her novel about them which she entitled *The Folks*.

The Folks is long—over seven hundred pages. As her earlier works show, Ruth Suckow was not given to the skillful interweaving of plot elements by which a lengthy novel is held together but preferred the short story or the short novel—what she called her own kind of fiction——in which a situation is created as background for the penetrating analysis of character. In *The Folks* she organizes her material into sections, one about each member of the family she portrays, each one a short narrative complete in itself. Yet each involves the other characters and their problems, angling in on them from diverse points of view. Thus by relating the Ferguson chronicle as a series of separate stories, Miss Suckow ingeniously puts her special gifts to use. She is enabled to study each individual character closely and to throw about the events involving each a particular and suitable coloration. *The Folks*, to be sure, is much more than a clutch of short pieces loosely held together by a common thread of continuity. Its narratives are densely interwoven, showing complex attitudes of family members toward one another, and presenting their differing reactions toward the same events.

All this is rendered against a richly detailed, realistic background which itself possesses great interest. Reliable as always in providng the minutiae to achieve a faithful re-creation of life within a certain tme and place, Miss Suckow in *The Folks* transcends her previous accomplishments as a Realist. She is more skillful than before in subordinating her descriptive materials to the purpose of the narrative. As a result, the wealth of detail enriches and unifies the work without calling attention to itself or suggesting the presence of the author.

II   *The Fergusons*

To represent "the folks," Miss Suckow created a typical small-town, middle-class family, the Fergusons of Belmond, Iowa. They live in a large frame house, set in an ample lawn, and enjoy the material comforts Mr. Ferguson's position in the bank affords them, augmented by country-fresh produce from the farm where the grandparents still live. Fred and Annie are upright, substantial pillars of the community and the Presbyterian Church. Their four children are well cared-for; they attend the public schools, and then go to college within the state. The parents feel they have prepared their offspring to advance in life beyond their own achievement. Mrs. Ferguson glories in the image of herself as a fortunate wife and mother that she consciously projects before other townspeople.

The children, however, are affected by changes that invade even their snugly insulated Midwest. Margaret, the older daughter, absorbs ideas from books, learns to scorn the provinciality of her home environment, and finally escapes to the Bohemianism of Greenwich Village. The younger son, Bunny, is attracted to Socialistic doctrines and marries the Marxist daughter of an immigrant laboring family. Dorothy, conventionally feminine, makes a romantic marriage and moves to California; but there her husband enters into money-making ventures regarded by the folks as dangerously unstable. Carl, the eldest and the closest to his parents' traditional ways, finds himself caught in the unhappy repressions of marriage with a coldly proper wife, herself the victim of puritanical restraints during her childhood.

Though the complications in *The Folks* are varied, all are dominated by a central theme of change which controls the structure of the novel. Change is at work in the world Miss Suckow shows us—natural, inevitable change that is part of the cosmic plan; historic change, reflected in the fading of pioneer patterns and the introduction of urban ways; and cataclysmic changes in the intellectual climate, the most startling and painful of all as new ideas disrupt the settled thinking of the folks. She records some of the most significant of these innovations in *The Folks*: the introduction of Freudian concepts, ideological revolts by "new" poets and fiction writers, Bohemianism and hedonism fostered by intellectual groups, increased credit buying and hazardous financing, Socialistic and Marxian thought.

Solidly posed against the forces of change, however, is the continuity represented by the folks. These Midwesterners have a settled permanence. Their roots are in the soil; they are attuned to nature and the universe. Mundane they may be, provincial, and even naïvely unsophisticated, but they possess an underlying folk wisdom. Faulkner's remark about another people of another region, "they will endure," seems equally applicable to them.

This is not to say that the folks are immune to change. The problems of aging are with them, the struggles between the older and the younger generations, and the slow, irrevocable passing of the years that bring illness, alteration, and death. They have to accept changes in the mores as pioneer customs give way to the more affluent, urbanized society to which they have "progressed." They suffer their share of frustration and sorrow. These inevitabilities give the book Ruth Suckow's characteristic note of sadness as she records the passing of the bright morning (noted in so many of her works) into the long shadows of afternoon which presage the night to come.

With this attitude, Ruth Suckow approaches her theme of change versus continuity in *The Folks*. The four Ferguson children confronting the forces of change in their separate ways furnish the *engagement*; and the account of their parents, set forth mainly in the introduction and conclusion, suggests the continuity that has existed from the beginning and that will endure. The young people's stories are not equal in weight. Bun's and Dorothy's are true short stories: the latter's, impressionistic and slight, after the manner of some of those in *Iowa Interiors*; the former's, more intellectually involved, with its antithesis of new and strange philosophies set over against the traditional thinking of the folks. The others, Carl's and Margaret's, are longer— novelettes, actually, each with several sections and covering a considerable segment of the protagonist's life.

III *Carl*

Carl's comes first, appropriately, since as the oldest he is most fully exposed to the old ways. He is the one of all the children whom the pattern of the folks' way of life seems to fit most perfectly. Besides, he is a born conformer. A football player and leader in the church young people's society, Carl is just the sort of fresh-faced, ingenuous youngster that girls and women adore. He has grown up with the approval of those around him, and he requires it. He instinctively follows the ways of the folks as a sure way to gain this approbation.

Carl naturally chooses Wilson College, a small Iowa denominational school, for his higher education, for in its environment he will continue to shine. Yet Carl's religious bent has something phony about it, he himself feels, even when he "got up to talk—quickly, warmly, persuasively—in the Young People's meeting, knowing that the leader always counted on Carl Ferguson to keep things going" (135). He feels himself "ardent, but unsure and somehow guilty." But though the idealism of Wilson College is milk-and-watery enough, it inspires in Carl a desire for community service. He enters the teaching profession and after a few years becomes a superintendent of schools.

Carl's marriage to Lillian White, daughter of another strongly Presbyterian family of Belmond, follows the pattern laid down by the folks. The Whites and the Fergusons are close family friends who customarily eat their Thanksgiving dinners together at one or another of their homes; the children are thrown together at all the church affairs and Young People's meetings. There are more dashing, more sexually alluring girls at high school than Lillian, but Carl feels that the folks expect him to marry his childhood companion. His grandfather points out to him, when he is feeling a bit uncertain, "to have a home and a good wife is the thing that matters. . . . Howard's girl [Lillian] is a fine, good girl. She ain't like so many of the young people these days. She's been a helper in the church since she was little. She'll stand by ye" (140).

Lillian is another product of the superimposing of the folk pattern. Her parents make their home with old Abner White, her grandfather, who forces his rigid Calvinism on the household. An only child, the little girl has lived timidly under his domination. All normal childish noise and spontaneous communication were forbidden. Even after her marriage to Carl whom she deeply adores, her grandfather's shadow stays with her and impresses her with guilt when she so much as laughs out loud. Yet her fragile blondeness has the charm of a cool, pink shell, like the one Carl's grandmother uses to hold back the door in her country farmhouse parlor. Lillian is a part of the old ways that Carl remembers from childhood. He can not imagine life without her.

But, in time, Lillian's frigidity, her coldly proper ways and hard, narrow integrity, repel her husband. When his associations with more worldly people suggest avenues of broader enjoyment of life, he considers giving up school work to take a position with a foundation in Philadelphia—a break with all she has known that terrifies Lillian. While the couple is on the brink of a serious rift during a summer vacation visit with the folks in Belmond, Lillian, ill and facing a third pregnancy, attempts suicide. The near-tragedy brings husband and wife together again, frightened and remorseful; but their reconciliation is saddened by the knowledge of their circumscribed situation. Lillian will cling to her fixed ways; nothing can change her. Yet Carl has to accept that their lives are inseparable. He gives up the Philadelphia venture, accepts a superintendency near his old home. As he considers this weakly compromising and expedient course, he tells himself with a flash of mature understanding, "Anyone was a child who had not learned for how little he counted" (251).

The story of Carl and Lillian shows a Freudian concern with the unhappiness resulting from childhood repressions. Lillian's is the more obviously scarred personality, but Carl also suffers from repressions. His younger brother Bun considers him "pretty much of a mess psychologically." Carl's attraction for girls and women, which he knows the family regards as dangerous and its exercise as sinful, is something he has always sternly suppressed. Later he reflects ruefully that part of his trouble has come about because "he has really, truly, ingenuously tried and desired to be good" (252). "Being good" means fitting himself into the family's pattern, and Carl has dutifully followed this course.

IV *Margot*

His sister Margaret, in contrast to Carl, is the black sheep of the Ferguson family, the odd one, the "dark sister." Ruth Suckow had always secretly sympathized with this sort of character in fiction; in Margaret, she gives her her full measure of attention. There are many of the author's own traits in Margaret—both have literary tastes and are clear-eyed observers and perceivers of fraud; but Margaret has a psychical twist. A notion that she is less loved than her parents' other children warps her relationship with her family and makes her an introvert. As a tiny child, she heard her mother tell a neighbor who was calling to see the new baby (Dorothy), "I'm glad she's fair. Margaret is so dark" (32). This statement she never forgot.

Margaret longs for the time her large dark eyes and luxuriant black hair will win their due appreciation; she detests the Belmond boys who trail after commonplace, blondish Mildred Summers, though she also scorns the one or two undesirable swains who seek her attention. At the same time she owns a perverse fascination for classmates whose shady backgrounds hint of mysterious knowledge beyond the pale of her conventional world. Her reading inflames her taste for the exotic. She becomes a devotée of Edna St. Vincent Millay, whose hedonistic values hold a novel appeal. Sophistication becomes her desideratum. She longs for New York, an environment where she imagines her individuality flowering and her beauty recognized. She visions herself, darkly seductive, as involved in a passionate love affair with a married man. Marriage for herself she disdains: "Regular marriage meant being like the folks, presenting a united front to the world, neither one doing as he or she wanted to do.... Marriage, Margaret had always thought of as *just the end*" (307).

Margaret finally escapes to New York through the ruse of taking library training at Columbia University. She becomes a denizen of the Village, changes her name to Margot, and eventually experiences the fulfillment of most of her early dreams, including those having to do with promiscuous affairs. At length she attracts the notice of a substantial married executive who rescues her from her precarious Village existence by finding her a good job with an advertising firm and a comfortable apartment with another business girl. In love at last, Margot nevertheless assures Bruce she has no desire for marriage; she only wants him to make her perfectly happy. Bruce complies. The two journey to the Southwest on an extended vacation trip. Margot finds inexpressible satisfaction in the desert country and the primitive charm of its inhabitants. She finds existence with Bruce in these surroundings natural and good. But "just when their love was at its best" (519), as she protests, Bruce tears himself away to return to his responsibilities. Margot is desolated.

After an unhappy stay with her parents in Belmond, she returns to New York to a barren career as an advertising copy writer. She discovers a substratum of Ferguson competence and shrewdness under the hedonism she has espoused. Just as she is about to reconcile herself to a single life devoted to making money, Bruce returns. He has sought her out because, as he confesses, he can not help himself, though he still can not offer marriage. The two resume their relationship, while tacitly recognizing a tarnished quality about it. Ironically, Margot is doomed to accept the ancient feminine role she has scorned, but without the solacing honor of wifehood. Irony, indeed, predominates in this account of the dark sister. Mistaken as she is, Margot has determination enough to get from life what she thinks she wants. To her, loss of innocence seems not too high a price to pay for knowledge and experience. Yet even so thoroughgoing a hedonist as Margot can not change her destiny as a woman—to yield to love and long to perpetuate it.

V *Dorothy*

Both Margaret and Carl suffer from the strictures imposed by the folks, but Dorothy reaps the rewards of community approval. Her marriage to Jesse serves as the subject of an idyllic section of the novel entitled "The Loveliest Time of the Year." In a family-centered society, no ritual is more important than marriage; and this Iowa June wedding shows the folks at their best. There are passages evoking the fresh summer sights and smells, the leafy green of the trees, "the peonies open in the sun." The plain but ample comfort of the house put in readiness, its "formal spaced cleanliness," the shining damask and silver on the table—all impart a feeling of occasion.

The story begins quietly with Jesse's arrival, his introduction to the folks, and their receiving him as a guest in the house. Then it is Dorothy's duty to take her young man on a walk to show him the town—the places and people who have been part of her growing-up years. Jesse is eager to take part in this ritual, for Dorothy's background as a small-town girl with a firmly rooted family life appeals to this orphaned, city-bred boy, the heir of a wealthy grandfather. It pleases him to peer into her "crazy old church," into the Sunday School room with its little chairs where his beloved used to sit, and to visit old bedridden Mrs. Bartlett, and receive her halting wishes and praise of his bride while Dorothy's beauty blooms more brightly in the mustiness of the dark bedroom. He is at his courtly best with Mrs. Bird who represents something special to Dorothy—a refined New England flavor lingering in the Iowa setting, "an old-fashioned, faintly literary, leisured side of Belmond, barely discernible in the composite of all its aspects" (268).

At home, friends drop in and are welcomed in the relaxed, easy hospitality of the Ferguson house—contemporaries of Dorothy's, full of their own hopes and plans, and old friends and neighbors of the folks who regard Dorothy as "one of our nicest girls." Margaret, at home after being expelled from the "normal" and not yet escaped to New York, looks on with envy mixed with triumphant pride as her little sister shines in this company; everything, she reflects, just falls into Dorothy's hands.

The acceptance of the bridegroom by the family is traditional, as is his introduction to the community shrines and personages. The folks' concern with continuity shows in their desire to make Dorothy's new husband one of them. By building up a regard for the establishment, they hope to increase its solidity and permanence. But, though the folks' part in the ritual is stressed, there is the contrapuntal theme of self-realization always present in Ruth Suckow's works. Dorothy's individuality, slight and passive though it is, is posed against the collectiveness of the folks. The account of the preparations that precede her wedding are given added dimension by the young bride's growing consciousness of what married love will mean. On the evening before their marriage, as Dorothy and Jesse embraced in the garden before separating for the night, this new knowledge suddenly envelops her:

> She had never known *this*. That was what she felt, as she went quickly and softly up the stairs. She felt with wonder how she was trembling. The world seemed shaken, broken apart, by shining, wonderful amazement. The features of her small, happy, known world had not really been changed for Dorothy by her "falling in love," or by the excitement of her engagement. They had been confirmed. But now she felt the ground move under her feet—she had even a sight of depths beneath it. Falling in love with somebody, engagement, marriage—these old terms, that she had always accepted, had a new meaning now. Terms, outlines, had suddenly become luminous. She had experienced a miracle. (286)

After that climactic moment, events move fatefully toward the wedding itself. A simple home ceremony—held on the lawn under the large maple tree where the children had had their swing and attended by the relatives, a few friends, and by Margaret and Bun—unite Jesse and Dorothy. Yet its simplicity has a ritual quality. The preparation of the bride by her women relatives—sister, mother, aunts—and her proceeding, pale and subdued in her sheer white gown, to meet her bridegroom; the exchange of vows; and finally the life-giving kiss that restores her to radiance have a timeless, human quality. Then, though the local and actual reassert themselves, events follow a universal pattern. The wedding breakfast, ample and delicious, served under the exacting supervision of Margaret, and finally the departure of the young married couple amid the farewells of their kinfolk and friends are typical of weddings of all times and places. Dorothy's wedding thus becomes a sort of symbol. Though it takes place in the midst of wartime upheaval and uncertainty, its traditional patterns reflect the underlying permanence of the institutions of family and home that is stressed anew each time young lovers exchange their vows in the presence of those near and dear to them. "Their world had gone back to its old innocence," says the author, "and everything was prosperous and fresh and sunlit again" (301).

VI *Bunny*

The complications in the story of Bunny, the son born late to the Fergusons, relate to the economic unrest following World War I. Bun travels West on a summer working venture, and becomes interested in the problems of immigrant laborers. His naturally quick sympathies touched by what he sees, he is susceptible on his return to the State University to the strange charms of a fellow student from the West, Charlotte Bukowska. Charlotte has been hitch-hiking across the country when the agricultural plenty of Iowa dazzles her eyes. She has been nursing a vague plan to engage in the cooperative farming movement in Russia, and she impulsively enrolls at the university with the idea of learning farming methods. The loneliness and fierce independence of this girl attracts Bunny, and soon the two are in love. Charlotte cares nothing for marriage, but at Bunny's insistence they are united in a civil ceremony.

Bunny's story is the account of the day he brings Charlotte home to the folks and tells them of his marriage. Its title "The Youngest" hides a touch of pathos, for in the maternal heart of Mrs. Ferguson "her baby" occupies a warm and special place.

The antithesis between this delicate, sheltered woman and the strange and uncouth immigrant girl she is asked to mother is the basis of the story. "Bourgeois" is of course the word Charlotte applies to everything about Bunny's home and family. His mother, on the other hand, knowing nothing of political ideology, has no vocabulary to describe Charlotte, though the author supplies the adjective "monolithic." To Mrs. Ferguson, the girl is rough, crude, unfriendly, and three years older than her son. For the first time, Bun observes on breaking his news, his mother fails to maintain her smooth front; she is utterly shattered. But after a distressing interval, she pulls herself together: "She had always so hated any suggestion that the whole family didn't stand together in perfect harmony!—and she couldn't bear that before Charlotte, this stranger. She managed to call up a wavering smile.... Then she kissed Charlotte gallantly, but in defeat, with her eyes full of tears" (559).

The concern with selfhood, the preciousness of the individual, is not missing from this story, either. It is apparent in Bun's sensitiveness to individuality—he has always sought to find in each of his girl associates the quality that makes her different. He feels that Charlotte has within her, though the hardships and violations of her girlhood have hardened her exteriorly, something untouched—"a pure, heroic center of her being." Charlotte's uniqueness attracts rather than repels him. "After Charlotte," he thinks, "all girls must forever seem trite" (552). She is like no one else he has ever known on earth.

Bunny's appreciation of Charlotte's quality is brought out in an exquisite little scene in which he shows her his family's farm— the one where his grandparents pioneered. It is an early spring day, raw and cool in the woods where they go to look for wild flowers. Though Charlotte declares she does not care for flowers, Bunny notices that "her touch showed a girl's own peculiar feeling for them—different from any man's—something intimate, personal, akin" (553). He holds out to her a bloodroot blossom, its orange red juice staining his fingers, its petals icy white and pure like Charlotte's own hidden personality, and says, "This is *your* flower."

Charlotte responds instantly. Tears come into her eyes, and Bun feels he knows what she is thinking:

His love for her seemed to make him almost clairvoyant at this

moment. He knew without words what she wanted to tell him—
that this was what she would rather have said to her than anything in the world. He had found her hidden symbol, and by
finding it, had given her to herself. She looked at him now, and
gratitude overflowed in the tears that brimmed her eyes, washing
out distrust. That color, that depth of pure blue, was imprinted
on his sight. Bun shyly touched her. Her whole splendid body
was yielding and soft. Humbly, with gratitude of his own, and
proudly, Bun felt the mutality of this embrace, different from
their others. How simple it had been!—the gift she had wanted.
(553)

All their problems are not solved in this moment of recognition, however. Sympathetic as he is with Charlotte and even with
her beliefs, Bunny is a child of the folks. He desires his marriage
to be as good as he can make it:

> His beloved would lead him along very strange ways; but he
> had to go, holding all the while to things of which she was
> unaware and which he had inherited, fusing the two in some
> difficult reconciliation . . . perhaps impossible. He seemed already
> to be far from the folks, although he would never relinquish his
> youthful love for them, his tender, comprehending appreciation.
> He and his bride were the inheritors of a stormy future, even
> here in the pleasant fastness of this middle-aged frame house on
> the familiar local street with the tall trees all up and down the
> asphalt. (565)

VII *Fred and Annie*

"Ruth Suckow's characters seem like people you have known
always," a critic has said.[3] Of none of them is this more true than
of the folks themselves, those typical Midwesterners, Annie and
Fred Ferguson, whose story is woven throughout those of their
children and comes to a climax in the final section of the novel.
Annie and Fred, like many young couples, start out under the
domination of the old folks. Fred's parents still own the family
farm and live on it, though their daughter Ella and her husband
Ben do most of the work; and they continue to exercise a strong
influence on the town Fergusons as well as on Ben and Ella.

Annie was a sought-after young school teacher when Fred
married her. She then leaves her own church for the Presbyterian, tries to conform to the strictness of Grandma and

Grandpa, and subjects her ways to her husband's according to
the code of fortunately married women. Fred is a good family
man, an adequate provider and careful householder; he is
"Scotch," in the commonly accepted sense of thrifty, stubborn,
and unimaginative. Annie, on the other hand, has German ante-
cedents and is generous and sentimental.

Actually, the two complement each other and make a successful marriage. In time the old folks die, and Fred and Annie
become "the folks." When they prosper, their family home is
remodeled according to prevailing standards of substantial comfort; their position among the best people in town is assured. It
is not until Bun's incredible marriage that their safe world seems
threatened by any hint of change, but then, all at once, they feel
it shaking. At first, Mrs. Ferguson is the more upset, but then
Fred senses alarming indications in his business that make him
decide to "close out his account" and retire from the bank. They
determine to close their house and go to California for the winter
—possibly to stay.

This trip to California is the ultimate goal of all well-to-do
Iowans. As the author points out earlier in her study entitled
"Iowa," young people go East for learning and culture; old people, West for health and recreation. Besides, the Fergusons'
daughter Dorothy and her family live in San Diego, and Annie's
sister Louie and her husband reside in Pasadena. The folks set
out with keen anticipation, in their Midwestern humility prepared to find California an Eldorado and to be impressed with
everything. Annie, especially, looks upon this trip as an opportunity to recapture her personal self, long lost in performing her
duties as wife and mother. "She could not say that her marriage
had not been happy, but her own separate life had gone down
beneath it. Maybe there was no self any more" (573).

Annie's hope to find herself again, unvoiced and only vaguely
felt, is at first ministered to by the exotic sights of California, its
fruits and flowers and fabulous vistas of city and shoreline. The
luxury of her sister's home soothes her. The extravagant devotion
of a new acquaintance who sees in her the faint residue of her
girlhood charm flatters her a bit. There are moments when she
hopes to leave Belmond forever behind and live always in this
wonderful lotus land. But her feelings are too nebulous to force
her to a clearly defined stand. The habit of yielding is too well-

established, or perhaps she hardly knows whether she really wants to break away from her old life.

The pathos in Annie's plight is sensitively conveyed. For her, as for myriads of other middle-aged women, it is too late for her to hope to make a career for herself or express herself artistically. Marriage and domesticity have demanded the submersion of self in favor of the goals of the family. Though she has gladly made the sacrifice, now she mourns what she has lost. On the other hand, Annie's fate, inexorable as it is, is clearly preferable to that of women who avoid sacrifice—as is brought out in the delineation of the character of Louie. Though inherently sweet-tempered, Annie's rich and childless sister has thrown a protective shell around herself. Louie's self-centered indifference hurts Annie when she tries to confide in Louie her misgivings about Margaret and her worries on behalf of her other children.

Old Mrs. Spencer of the banking family in Belmond is another example. The sisters spend an afternoon with her out of respect for the Spencers' standing as Fred's former employers. The old lady has abdicated the traditional role of sacrificial conformity and is living out her remaining days in California "only to please herself," as she triumphantly tells the younger women. She recommends a similar course to Annie. But her existence seems a pitiable one, with only servants for companions and the most salacious of movies to fill her hours. Gaudily painted and bedizened, she retains but a shred of the stately dignity of her Belmond days.

Annie does not protest Fred's decision to return to Belmond at the beginning of summer. She has no desire to become like old Mrs. Spencer and knows she will return to take up her role in Belmond unchanged. That smooth front Margaret denounces as hypocritical has become habitual. It is required of her as her contribution to the well-being of the folks at large in her standing as reputable wife of a leading citizen.

Fred's responsibility is taken for granted of course. Iowa folks expect a man to assume the load—of supporting and caring for his family, of being a mainstay in business, of contributing money and effort to his church and to civic groups. Though Fred has left the bank, he has not relinquished his sense of duty. When the report comes that the other bank in Belmond has failed, its manager disappearing under a cloud of suspicion, Fred feels he must get home and "see to things." His responsibility is closely linked to his integrity, though the two are not exactly identical. His brother-in-law Henry, who shrugs his shoulders upon hearing of the defection of the other banker, implies that "Hoagland was wise to get out while the getting was good"(674). Fred, however, "never liked to make promises he was not reasonably sure of being able to keep." He does not care for the "new way of doing business."

The Fergusons' homecoming brings more disillusionment to Fred than to Annie, who understands little of changing business conditions. Fred has always looked to the future of his town with hope that it will be better than the past. Now the future seems doubtful; the small, conservative place will do well to hold its own. His children, too, Fred has expected to "do better" than he has; now he sees that they may not do as well. Though the family farm is as richly productive as ever, the renters are discontented and utter new complaints about their lot. Fred thinks of some of Bun's notions; and, though he formerly considered them heresy, he now reflects that maybe "land so good oughtn't to belong to any one man, particularly if he wasn't going to live there" (719).

Fred may be said to set the tone of *The Folks;* he is most completely in accord with prevailing ways. He is practical and materialistic (his son Carl comments that "Dad was religious but not exactly idealistic"), downright, plain, and honest. His speech reflects these qualities and his interior monologues are couched in characteristic Midwestern phrases. He looks upon Iowa as his "stamping grounds"; he feels he is "blowing himself" on the dates and "stuff" to send back home; a well-to-do person is spoken of as "well-fixed": he is uncertain about Margaret—"if she was carrying on, as Mama seemed to think—."

The Folks is not Fred's book, however, in the sense that *Babbitt* is George Babbitt's. The femininity of its author completely dominates *The Folks*; it is unquestionably a domestic chronicle. One critic complained that many of its details are "vulgar";[4] certainly they are homely. There is a great amount of emphasis on such homemaking concerns as meals, clothes, furniture, gardens, pets, and plumbing. Even Fred most often reveals himself in his role as householder—he is mending the seat of his children's swing in the opening scene of the novel and at its close he is sniffing about his basement for possible mice.

In *The Folks* the speech and actions of all the characters, in fact all the details of the narrative, merge so naturally into the structure as to be scarcely noticeable in themselves. They simply impress one as being exactly right and true. Minor characters—and there is an ample gallery of them—possess the same rightness. Mrs. Christianson, actually a domestic helper but more like one of the family, is an example. So is the second Mrs. White, who is heartily disapproved of by the folks, but who is entertained with her husband for Carl and Lillian's sake. The following passages from the Carl section present her unforgettably:

> Mrs. White sat fat and heavy in the light mahogany and cane rocker, with one foot in a painful patent leather slipper slightly extended, and from time to time delicately touched her nose with an embroidered gift handkerchief with an air of great social majesty. . . .
> Cake and grape juice were passed, as a mild compensation for not having asked the Whites to dinner. Forrest, with very bright eyes, watched the way Mrs. White ate her cake, delicately crumbling it before she picked up the crumbs—as if there were a regal superiority in this method of doing it that committed her to nothing. After the refreshments were eaten she rose; and Howard then had to rise too. . . .
> "Had a very nice evening," Mrs. White murmured with immense sedateness that seemed to conceal some mysterious feeling of offense. (186-87)

Miss Suckow's vocabulary, to quote her husband again, has a way of becoming the thing it signifies; and this protean quality of her language is one of her distinctive stylistic charms. Two words that she uses repeatedly to describe the Iowa small town way of life are "local" and "retail." As the Fergusons drive into Belmond after their trip to California, "the town looked small and *local* under the heaviness of the trees" (686). Margot feels like an outsider when she attends a Rotary picnic with her parents: "The voices sound like voices on the stage. And yet everything seemed *local* and small and actual" (473). When Carl visits his father in the new bank building, he "missed the heavy *retail* reliability of the other bank" (194). In these sentences the reader hears the word with Miss Suckow's special inflection giving it the very meaning she wishes. "Local" has all the connotations of the local paper that carries the folksy and trivial local news and of the local train that stops at every little burg. "Retail" holds the image of a small-town storekeeper with sateen sleeve guards and a personal knowledge of all his customers.

The pleasure that Ruth Suckow offers in her fiction, says Josephine Herbst, is chiefly that of recognition. This characteristic is most specifically true, of course, for her Iowa readers; but it holds to some extent for all Midwesterners. They acknowledged her authenticity and took pleasure in it. But, though *The Folks* was popular—probably the best-liked of her books—it was not wholeheartedly favored by her fellow Iowans. She herself related that an old school friend whom she visited in Des Moines during her early career "scolded her because her books were not the kind people would want to read."⁵ "Iowa people didn't care for her brand of realism," Professor Clyde Tull of Cornell College stated.⁶

Probably not her Realism so much as her staunch anti-Romantic treatment was the actual culprit. Her truthful representation of tangible details in *The Folks* could be expected to bring only delight tinged with nostalgia to any good Iowan; but, as in most of her work, the underlying meaning was too fraught with universal sadness to make for what many people call "pleasant reading." As usual, the author refuses the reader the romantic happy ending he craves, and furthermore she derides her characters for indulging in the same impossible dreams. Though Margaret's vision of life is "modern" and hedonistic, it is still based on the romantic belief that she can master her own fate. Carl's is the old-fashioned faith in goodness inherited from the nineteenth-century church and schoolroom. Fred's chauvinistic optimism has romantic overtones too, as does Annie's sentimental backward yearning for her dreamy, water-coloring young self. None of their air castles, the author makes us aware, will come true.

Yet the author of *The Folks* is no thunderous Nay-sayer. While scorning either to prettify or to falsify life's inevitabilities, she yet affirms a steady faith in the worthwhileness of existence. There is much good in life. Margot's dubious situation is made bearable by love; Carl, once he has accepted the little he counts for, values his family the more; Fred still has his comforts and "Mama"; and Annie solaces herself with cherished memories during the gentle evening of her days.

No incidents of individual heroism spark *The Folks*. The quest for self-fulfillment through experiment with new patterns of thought and behavior meets opposition in the family-community insistence on continuity and conformity; but the outcome of the struggle produces only quiet acceptance tinged with sadness— the distinctive emotional coloration of the author. When she wrote *The Folks*, she had not yet surely fixed upon an amalgam that would resolve her people's predicament and make tolerable their burdens of responsibility and sacrifice. That was to be the object of her search in the several books to come.

On the surface, then, *The Folks* might appear to be a prosaic chronicle of ordinary people undergoing commonplace experiences. It has been branded as "dull," though most readers would grant to its plentiful flow of incident and vivid characterization at least the humble accolade of interesting. (In Margaret's story there is even that touch of the meretricious!) But *prosaic* is not a word one likes to apply to the culminating work of an author who entered fiction by way of the lyric poem and whose avowed purpose was to capture the moment of beauty so that its distinctive quality need never be lost. Nor does the word fairly describe this novel which possesses much the same winning quality as the lyric short stories of *Iowa Interiors*. Like the early stories, this entire long work is imbued with the author's characteristic sense of place or, as she designated it, "the poetry of place."

Miss Suckow's gift for the miraculous small touch that evokes entire reality, which has been noted, is present throughout *The Folks*, but it operates in a larger scope as the author realizes Iowa in its place in the continent and even in the universe. The description of Fred Ferguson's responses on returning to his home state from California is a case in point:

> He had a feeling of exaltation as they drove along—up and down, gently up and down, on the great smooth billows of the rolling country. Talk about the ocean! The land was just as big. The rich earth that spread on every side was rounded by the sweep of the globe. . . .
>
> Coming into a town, they rode through green caverns of shade. There was a sense of teeming thickness in the close-built streets under the heavy trees. The leaves were so dense that a blackness lay at the heart of the foliage. . . . It gave the feeling of having

come into the warm, unconscious, breathing interior of the
mighty continent. (685).

At the end of Dorothy's wedding day, as the young couple
prepared to drive away, this passage occurs: "It was still full
daylight. The familiar lawn, the cream-colored house standing
there, were transfigured. It seemed as if the whole earth, at
this most beautiful time of the year, was in bloom for the wedding" (301).

In its over-all aspect, *The Folks* resembles a variegated tapestry; it illumines in detail the lives of small-town, middle-class
people. To shift the figure, it might also be likened to a fugue,
its themes combined into a complex whole as they are stated in
various keys and tonal patterns. Individuality is set over against
collective existence; change against continuity. But the likeness
to a tapestry suits it best, for the controlling figure the author
repeatedly employs is the natural one of light and shade. The
mornings are bright and sunny; the late afternoons throw long
shadows in the grass. The shadows, however, represent only the
illusion of change upon the everlasting permanence of the earth.
And the changes in one human life span, however saddening as
the shades of age close in, also seem illusory when viewed
against the total permanence of the ongoing chain of generations.

The well-worn figure of light and shade takes on special meaning when applied to the Iowa scene. The dense shade (black at
its center) from the heavy leafage suggests the product of the
region's incomparably fertile soil when it is warmed into fecun-
dity by the passionate sun. All Miss Suckow's works are pervaded
by this sense of teeming productivity. But in *The Folks*, more
than in any of the others, it is made to convey cosmic overtones.

In other ways as well, *The Folks* reveals expansion of its
author's imaginative power, calling for revision of the judgment
previously made that her genius consists not so much in imagination as in enlightened perceptiveness. Though she abjured
reliance on symbols as artificial, one can detect in this book a
stress on certain objects and sensory details that endows them
with meaning beyond their denotation. Red roses, Margaret's
chosen flower, enhance her dark beauty and stand for her flam-
ing desire for love and life. Lillian, however, is like a cool, pink
shell. The hard click of their heels on the city pavement signifies

the arid heartlessness the author attributes to modern business and professional women. Grandpa and Grandma's old rock house on the farm stands for old-time rural virtues of plainness and firmness.

As previously stated, *The Folks* is in many ways Miss Suckow's crowning achievement. Dorothy Canfield Fisher wrote Miss Suckow enthusiastically upon the publication of *The Folks*: "It's great! It's simply wonderful! It's perfect! You must be feeling proud and happy and serene." She assured her friend that "The New York Village section is *just as good* as the rest—better than anybody else has ever done that, it seems to me." She reported telling her husband "Of course it has its limitations as every art form has its limitations. But granted those, Ruth has filled her form with pure gold, heaped up, pressed down, running over. And oh the use of detail—combined with luminous light—Vermeer-like, nothing less! It makes you feel just as Vermeer does —a sort of anguish of pleasure in the exactitude and yet the transfigured quality—."[7]

These comments of Dorothy Canfield are hastily penned encomiums, not a critique; but they capture the character of *The Folks*: its brilliance combined with its integrity suggests the worth of pure gold. Many readers agreed with Carl Van Doren that nothing finer had ever been done with this material, the life of the Midwest on the farms and in the small towns. This judgment has not changed with the years. To the end of her life, Miss Suckow received letters from admirers concurring with it; many expressed the wish that the book might be reissued in a popular edition, thus making more available to the public its important representation of American life and character.

VIII *After* The Folks

If the earlier works of Ruth Suckow—*Odyssey, The Bonney Family*, and *Children and Older People*—tend to draw heavily on childhood memories and to show us the author's world through the eyes of a child, and if the somewhat later novels, *Cora* and *The Kramer Girls*, are imbued with feminism and view life with a woman's bias, *The Folks* marks the development of the author as an observer of the entire culture. In it she shows a satisfying artistic maturity. On reading it and recognizing this development, though the reader might have sighed with regret as it end-ed (as in the case of all really good books), there was the happy anticipation that more of the same quality could be expected from its author. But somehow her career failed to develop in quite this expected way; and, though the works that came subse-quently from her pen possessed their own kind of excellence, there were no achievements similar to *The Folks*. Many reasons might be advanced to explain this outcome, but whether the truth lies in any one of them, or in a combination, is only to be guessed.

In the first place, there is always the obvious explanation that the author has mined out this particular vein of ore. Her purpose had been to represent her people in the commonplace tenor of their everyday lives, and in *The Folks* she had done this with a virtuosity she could not expect to surpass. Similar treatments of the same sort of existence would have been simply repetitious; Moreover, to one of her exploratory and ongoing type of mind, it would have been unthinkable to harp over and over on the same string.

Second, the personal life of Miss Suckow underwent a change at this time, as she and her husband returned to Cedar Falls, Iowa, where they made their home for the next several years. Miss Suckow did not by any means sink into anonymity during this period, for she continued to visit writers' conferences where she talked helpfully to young authors and spoke out for the future of Midwestern literature. She and her husband occupied an honored place in the Cedar Falls community, and Miss Suckow was virtually writer in residence in her relationship with the Iowa State College English staff who loved and respected her profoundly. But, third, her family responsibilities increased dur-ing her residence in Cedar Falls. The illness of her husband's father had brought them back to Iowa in the first place; family business matters now devolved upon her husband. Her own father, who lived some miles away in Alden, was still preaching, though growing increasingly frail.

And, fourth, Ferner Nuhn, also a writer, was applying himself during these years to a work of his own, a study of the move-ment of cultural influence from East to West in the United States. This was brought out in 1942, entitled *The Wind Blew from the East: A Study in the Orientation of American Culture.*

Concurrently, Mr. Nuhn interested himself in the arts, and served as president of the Cedar Falls Art Association for some six years. Life for Miss Suckow in this period, then, was busy and intellectually and artistically absorbing, but diffused in a number of diverse directions. Her thinking tended to become more philosophical and analytical; there was less reliance on the springs of personal inspiration, and her writing reflects this change.

Only a few short stories by her appeared in magazines during the 1930's; two were included in the collection *Some Others and Myself* in 1951, but several have never been reprinted. One of the most thought-provoking appeared in *Harper's* in 1939 under the title "What Have I."[8] Its grasp of contemporary social problems and its psychological penetration are so remarkable as to cause regret that it has been left to languish in the back files. It also shows us in Winifred Serles a figure who, like Melville's Bartleby, can be understood in the light of the author's own situation and frustrations.

In "What Have I" the Depression is over, and prosperity has returned to Iowa. The setting is a Mississippi River town, whose people are descendants of the old families of the region. Winifred Serles, the protagonist, is a beautiful, pampered, middle-aged woman, the daughter of a highly esteemed pioneer doctor and his well-loved wife. Winifred is herself the wife of a successful lawyer and the mother of happily married children. After a serious illness, followed by a winter in Florida, she is at home again, surrounded by devoted friends and seemingly endowed with every blessing heart can wish. We see her lapped in luxury as, modishly dressed, she is being driven to the spring meeting of her club at an historic old country home, a gathering place since her girlhood. The beautiful old Bliss place, built by a Civil War general, seems part of a timeless world. Statues of Civil War heroes stand about the grounds. Lilacs bloom in a lofty hedge. Everywhere is leisure, space, and quietude.

The club members appear gay and smart in their new spring outfits; but their chatter is disquieting. It deals with modern unease, discontent with government controls, and trouble with domestic help. One woman exclaims petulantly, *"Don't* let's talk about politics, economics, labor troubles, or war or *mention* the President or the WPA. Let's not bring such things in to the Club. I make it a motion!"* (135). Winifred feels her happiness at being

back with "the girls" undermined by the consciousness of opening rifts. Worst of all is her knowledge of her husband Alton's
shameful betrayal of an old friend in order to protect a rich
client involved in a municipal graft scandal.

When Winifred asked for explanations, Alton had made it clear
that her sheltered, expensive way of life was not one that could
be paid for by quixotic loyalty to unimportant persons. He ges-
tured toward their luxuriously furnished home: "This didn't
come from playing ball with Frank Hood! Not in a town like
this, with a man like Grover Hurd where he is in this town."
He went on to say: "When I married you, and promised to love
and cherish you, and told your dad that was going to be the
main object of my life, I meant just what I said. I meant to do
the most I could for my family and myself. For you first. All
right. I have. And I will. You can depend on that. But you can
take it that way or not at all" (132).

The scene with Alton sears her memory as she sits among her
friends. It occurs to her that most of the other women are
also hiding disillusionment and unhappiness. A talented young
woman plays a piano solo, modern and dissonant. To Winifred,
the music is disrupting, though played with casual expertness.
Later the young pianist is addressed by a club member.

"How do you do it, you wonderful child, with your beautiful
house, and everything else? And you and Glenn never miss out
on any good times. I think that's *so* wonderful."

Gail answered drily, "I don't keep it up." Another woman
broke in.

"My dear, why say that? Now don't set your standards impos-
sibly high! We don't ask you to be absolutely pro-*fes*-sional."

"I know you don't," Gail answered, even more drily. (135)

A number of other disturbing indications mar the afternoon
as the guests amble about the grounds, chat, and partake of a
lavish tea. Then Winifred is driven back to town, dropping one
of the younger women at her house on the way. This house is in
the wrong part of town, on the river bottom, but boasts a run-
down picturesqueness admired by its arty owners. A glimpse of
the underprivileged residents of the region gives Winifred an
uneasy feeling. She welcomes with relief the exclusiveness of her
own neighborhood and her tasteful home. But her troubles are

unresolved. She can take no pleasure in her lovely clothes or possessions. She wonders "whether she really has anything."

This multi-leveled story is laden with complexities and contrasts. The social felicities taking place in its dream-like setting cover a maze of cross-purposes and contemporary stresses and strains. On one level it offers a vivid picture of middle-class Midwestern society recovering its aplomb after the extremities of the Depression. Shafts of satire highlight the characterizations of its well-heeled matrons. But the particular problem of her central character is always Miss Suckow's chief concern. Winifred Serles is being forced to examine her marriage in the light of a new and frightening awareness of its conditions. Her being regarded as a mere chattel by her husband—she recalls that during the aforementioned scene "he glared at her as if she were only part of the surroundings" (132)—echoes the author's earlier feminism. But the problem Winifred is facing has deeper implications: it has to do with right and wrong and with her freedom to choose the right and to act in accordance with her choice. This is a freedom she has always taken for granted. Her parents, "some of the very best people who ever lived—the kindest people, the most conscientious" (127), have taught her their way of life. In the easy democracy of an earlier day, their dealings with neighbors and household help were on a person-to-person basis. Now all is changed. Relationships are depersonalized, with the government stepping in, even between employer and employed.

Winifred "felt as if she were a tiny, soft, tame animal that had got helplessly into some gigantic trap" (135). Her distress is increased when the aged handyman at the Bliss mansion addresses her by her maiden name—Miss Wallingford. She is reminded that she is indeed trying to live by the outmoded code she has learned as Miss Wallingford. As Mrs. Serles she has every luxury but that of integrity. Deprived of it, she piteously cries, "What have I?"

The author betrays in this story her discontent with current trends; little encouragement offered the artist to perfect his accomplishment and a weakening of the moral tone in business and community life. Her longing for the simplicities of an earlier day she is soon to show in an engaging light in the pages of her forthcoming novel *New Hope*.

CHAPTER 6

Memories

T IS PROBABLE that *New Hope* had been germinating for
some time as its author pursued her serious writing at a
slowed-down pace; for a letter to her publishers, dated February
20, 1941, assures them that "New Hope will be in your hands
quite fairly soon."[1] As different as possible from *The Folks, New
Hope* is quite as notable in its way and even more unforgettable
as an adventure of the imagination. When it appeared, during
the early and darkest days of World War II, its title struck a
welcome note of contrast that the book itself sustained. Ferner
Nuhn, always apt in judging his wife's writings, spoke of it as
"a kind of gem,"[2] a phrase that suits well its small perfection and
the bright clarity of its composite picture.

I   New Hope

New Hope, a small community newly established at the beginning of the present century on the western border of Iowa, is
re-created through the experiences of a little boy and girl during
the two-year period of their idyllic friendship. Through the eyes
and thoughts of Clarence Miller are related some of the high-
lights of his association with Delight, whose father spends a short
period in New Hope as the minister of Clarence's church. The
two children, about six or seven at the time, are involved in a
variety of home, church, and community doings; for Clarence
belongs to a large active household: his father is a banker who
is also a civic leader, and his three grown-up sisters are attractive
social belles. These two households, the Millers and the Greenwoods, are pivotal centers of activity, spreading outward to include the church and then, less importantly, the town and the
surrounding countryside. The chapter headings suggest this basis
of selection: Following the opening one, "Arrival," they continue

with "The Church," "The Town," "The Countryside," and "The Parsonage." The rest are given over to occasions that loom large in Clarence's memory and are entitled "Festivals," "The Big Crowd," "May Day," "The Turn of the Year," "Commemoration," "The Call," and "Exodus."

An interesting resemblance can be noted between these chapter titles and those of *Walden*—which records another significant sojourn of two years by singling out salient impressions and marking the progression of the seasons. A further likeness, reduced to miniature, of course, is present in the underlying purpose. Just as *Walden*'s author insisted that he sought, in closeness to nature, to learn about life, so the author of *New Hope* is revealing, through the thin veil of allegory, what life becomes for a little boy when Delight is part of it. The movement of the novel, though quiet, is perceptible—it is episodic rather than interwoven—and at its ending its young protagonist is changed.

It is this quality of youth recaptured that distinguishes *New Hope*. Bright morning light suffuses it, from the arrival of the Greenwoods at the railroad station to their departure from the same station two years later. To Clarence, the interval seems forever set apart—the time of Delight. As the train bears her away, "the little boy somehow sensed that this marked the end of a time. The morning world where the two children had lived together, encircled by communal closeness . . ." (341). The suggestion inherent in the little girl's name has prompted many readers to see the work entirely as a parable—as a restatement of the Wordsworthian concept that a child's world is delightful chiefly because he sees it through fresh, unclouded eyes. Some have applied the analogy specifically to America, once fair and shining with promise, now darkened and troubled by war. "This is what we were; this is what we can be again," are the words of one of the book's champions.[3] Viewed in this way, *New Hope*'s small-town image comes to stand for the better world we all desire.

There are unquestionably elements of Utopia in *New Hope*. The "communal closeness" of the little place is one. As Dave Miller, Clarence's father, tells the minister, all the people are needed in New Hope—each contributes his talents to the building of the town. When the Miller brothers saw the need for a bank, they sold their grocery store and went into banking. Old Mr. Broadwater, who came to live with his married daughter, took up paperhanging first to help his daughter in the establishment of her home, and now keeps it up because the town needs his services. "It takes all kinds," Dave is fond of saying.

This primitive democratic quality has nothing of institutional communism about it. Mutuality is its keynote. The people share a common concern for the welfare of their community and a vital faith in its future. They joy in every sign of its growth and progress and involve themselves in it. In the summer evenings they go in groups to visit the new houses under construction, most of them being built for young couples about to marry. With the children in tow, they inspect the raw, unfinished rooms; and Clarence and Delight visualize adored members of the "big crowd" starting their family life in these surroundings. These communal visitings have a simplicity about them. The people's ways hold something of the flavor of the old frontier days, but they are gentler. Hospitality is a part of them—what meals! what cooking the Greenwoods enjoyed when they visited the Millers! But a touch of plainness and bareness is suggested, too.

The optimistic faith in the future which distinguishes the little Western Iowa community is epitomized in the attitude of Dave Miller, a born promoter, and by the less secular but equally forward-looking Mr. Greenwood. "You wouldn't believe any town could make so much progress in so short a time," Dave exults. "And we're just at the beginning" (24). Mr. Greenwood's confidence spreads to the whole human race. "Mankind will solve all these problems in time," he asserts (95), when the farmers talk about the unsureness of rainfall. His feeling for the land has a mystical flavor. Riding through the countryside on his bicycle as he makes his rural calls, "he would feel drunk with the sense of boundlessness." And it was new! It had never been used for settled dwellings. "That gave it its own virtue," he declares. "New Hope wasn't built upon ruins. Their town was the first. It started history here" (201).

The chronicle of New Hope continually stresses the virtue of newness. Not only are the town and its buildings recently built, but "the smell of the earth is new—the light blue sky has the freshness of morning." Evil on the other hand is described as "ancient." When the church janitor is accused of stealing the collection money, his mien takes on the ancient air of the "old, low level" to which he has fallen (237). The old is always suspect, even in Clarence's mother, with her proneness to gossip, her folk adages, and her timidity tinged with superstition. She has that "female grossness" that Miss Suckow shows herself sensitive to in other works, and that is fundamental, linked to the earthy, generative forces. When Clarence comes from school on raw winter days he finds his mother's cronies in the kitchen, gossiping over cake and coffee: "Coming from outside, the room seemed to him like a cave, thick with warm odors, aroma of coffee and fresh spicecake, and the scorching smell of ironing. The cave was full of womenfolks gathered around the kitchen table. In that close atmosphere the sense of female was enough to knock anybody down" (181).

The children themselves dwell in a sort of Eden. Clarence feels this way about it: "There was always this excitement in being with Delight—a naturalness that was tinged with magic. Whatever they did together was fun. They didn't need anybody else if they could be together. Delight said they must count all the fence posts or the Old Witch would get them. Clarence had never quite dared to ask what the Old Witch was like. But it seemed to him she was somewhere now, in a darkness like a storm cloud, in the golden dusty air above the faded cornfields. A shiver went down his backbone" (87).

Delight suggests the game to play in Uncle Andy's cornfields on this same occasion—a drive into the country to spend the day. To the children, the corn shocks look like little wigwams. In their game, Clarence is Hiawatha, and goes on a hunting expedition with "pretend" bows and arrows; Delight is Minnehaha and stays at the "wigwam." When he returns she is sitting out in front of it cross-legged, singing the song they learned in school— "Ea - wah - yea, - my little owlet." She has let down her braids of long fair hair in order to look more like Minnehaha.

In summer, when they play along the creek, Delight is Queen Isabella and Clarence is Columbus and goes exploring—farther than he ever dared go before. Delight also tells Clarence most of the stories in her books (she has learned to read before she goes to school).

in her eager voice, speaking for all the characters, deep and awful for the Old Witch and the ogre, in sweet, tiny tones for Tom Thumb and Thumbelinda, [*sic*] in squeaky tones for the brownies and marvellous whispers for the fairies. Delight was steeped in fairy tales. She moved surrounded by the golden and starlit glimmer of their enchantment even on the long, straight boardwalks of New Hope; and the characters, Snow White, the Easter Rabbit, and Snow Queen, were just as familiar to her as Ollie Jenks and Mr. Groundhog and the "characters" in town were to Clarence. He knew the fairy and legend people too, now; but only when he was with Delight. They were real to him when she told him about them. (119)

Clarence sometimes thinks about the days before Delight came. They are "dark and vaguely troubled in his memory," as if they "belonged to a time before he was awake—almost before he was born" (342). The little girl has indeed awakened something new in him. Not physical desire, which would be incongruous, but a vision of a world made "various and beautiful and new." Clarence's is a fairly sluggish sensitivity, it must be admitted, but Delight's creative spark is strong and vital, and the circumstances of New Hope are favorable. Once his imagination is touched into being, everything is changed for him.

Miss Suckow wrote her publisher that she hoped to bring out in *New Hope* "a certain poetic quality of past and present mingling."[4] In her simple phrase is implied the paradoxical union of the old and the new that she so successfully contrived. There is, of course, a sense in which the oldest is forever new. Myth and legend have a perpetual freshness about them, breathing of early, early times when the world was young. This is the quality of *New Hope*. It is a parable, surely, though probably not primarily intended to suggest a return to "the good old days" of our country. Its meaning would seem to be far more universal—the innocent freshness of an uncorrupted time that allowed the liberation of the spirit through imagination.

In achieving this purpose, the author set herself the task of evoking a reality more real than actuality, pictured with the clean, bright edges and with larger-than-life effect of cherished memories, partaking of the nature of dreams. Her Iowa scenes are clearer, more down-to-earth in this work than in any of the others, and they bear no trace of her characteristic wistfulness since these children of hers had not yet learned of sorrow. But the book's clarity is not its premier achievement. That lies in the miraculous transition from the actual to the abstract that she repeatedly renders impressionistically, but without loss of clarity, through the mind of a child.

Two examples may stand for the many that the book contains. The first is of the Christmas Eve that Clarence and Delight share on occasion, pre-eminent among the "Festivals" of the New Hope church and community. In the beautifully decorated church, with its glittering Christmas tree, the young people (of "the big crowd") first present a cantata, the product of many weeks of diligent rehearsing. Then gifts are given out—many intriguing parcels to Clarence's glamorous sisters, apples and hard candy to the primary children—and finally the minister rises and reads in clear tones the Christmas story from the New Testament:

> Clarence listened, wriggling in his seat. For the first time, this was not just a reading from the scriptures that came at a certain point in the program. Meaning shone from the words, and shone around them, in the scent of the evergreens and the unsteady candlelight—surrounded by the white silent glitter of great snow-fields, great smooth billowing acres of winter snow. Clarence felt the awesomeness of that shining immensity that lay all around them outside the windows. But he and Delight were here together, in the midst of their own community—Delight in her warm, red dress, with her light gold hair; and from their happy closeness, holding their presents, the meaning of the words spread out to everyone in the church. It was true, Clarence thought with joyous wonder—he was happy, he hated nobody, not even Willie Schnitts. He felt "on earth peace, good will toward men." (157)

The other example is the closing scene at the station with the townspeople gathered to bid goodbye to the minister's family:

> The train had begun pulling out. Merrill (who had gone into the train to find seats for the Greenwoods) leaped off just in time. Clarence ran a short futile distance along the wooden platform. He was living still in the moment of parting, still saw Delight's face looking out at him, her shining eyes open . . . but all the while she was being carried farther and farther away. The train windows flashed more and more rapidly. Then came the last swaying coach. The rails were left humming in the summer heat. The water tank showed in stark structure at a short distance down the tracks. People were still in the attitude of waving

good-bye; until now they realized that the train was gone. . . .

New Hope seemed empty and tame. A light had gone from it—Clarence could almost see the magical light shining even now ahead of the train, rushing on into the unexplored distance. . . .

It could not last. It was not here any more. Those who could see only by that unstained morning light must push beyond and look for it elsewhere; keep on looking for it elsewhere, always elsewhere. The glow was transitory.

Yet it had been; it existed. . . . He had come to feel the force of that experience, the need born of a fortunate start: to renew the sequence and finish out the early promises in fuller light and mature form. He faced the austere, enlarged demand to place completion far ahead, if necessary, beyond his own time; beyond any time he could see or realize; but to find his individual fulfillment in acting in accordance with its realization. (542)

Miss Suckow carries Clarence's reflections further than customary in these final paragraphs, for she had dispensed with the sequel she first projected and in which she had planned to make her concluding points. She came to feel that the "poetic mingling" she was striving for would be more surely attained by the method she adopted, though these are "long, long thoughts" for a seven-year-old.

Most of the time Clarence and Delight are simply two completely real and engaging youngsters—unquestionably Ruth Suckow's happiest juvenile creations. Together with all the *New Hope* characters, some of them recognizable Suckow types, they have a peculiarly lustrous quality overlaying their reality. Obviously they were real children to their author, too, and not mere figures in an allegory. To a friend with whom she carried on a lifetime correspondence, sharing news and comments about family matters, among other things, Miss Suckow wrote, not long after the publication of *New Hope*: "Your account of Carol, your daughter, and her marriage I want to keep. I thought that Carol and her husband were working out in actual life, and in maturity, the kind of love of which the children in my story had only a foretaste."[5]

To the same friend, who had known the Reverend Suckow in former days, she wrote, in an answer to a query as to whether Ruth's father had been the model for the Reverend Greenwood of *New Hope*: "Of course some of my father's personal charac-

teristics—his eyes, his active, springing walk, and his tastes—
are in the picture of the minister—and the spirit of his preaching, the import as I have understood it. . . . But the characters
in New Hope have only points of resemblance to actual people—
their lives are not the same."⁶

II "A Memoir"

Though the author insisted that the characters in *New Hope*
were not re-creations of actual persons, nevertheless, when she
wrote a tribute to her father in *A Memoir,* her representations of
him in his young days and of the church at Hawarden are in
many ways identical with the descriptions in *New Hope.*

Ruth Suckow wrote this memoir to be included in the volume
of seven short stories she was preparing to publish in 1952.
When a long short story (or novelette) entitled *Sequel by a
Later Hand,* which dealt with a family conflict between a son
and his parents at the time of World War I, did not prove satisfactory to Miss Suckow, she decided to reserve it for further
work and to write instead what had been in her mind for some
time—an autobiographical sketch centered about her own upbringing in the home of a liberal minister. She was eager to
compose this as a tribute to her father. Their closeness during
the last few years of his life had affected her deeply; her imagination had subsequently been stirred by her creating in *New
Hope* the character of the minister who resembled him. The
years since his death in 1939 had brought his daughter a full
appreciation of the Reverend Suckow's character and attain-
ments, so that the writing of *A Memoir* proved to be truly a
labor of love.

The purpose of *A Memoir* is to refute the widely held belief
about ministers' children and their rearing. As the author says
at the outset, "I am impelled, in a sense, to offer testimony"
(173). This testimony is her assessment of the positive values
in an upbringing such as hers. Whereas ministers' children are
frequently presumed to have been reared in a harsh religious
climate, resulting in their later rebellion and frustration, "I grew
up," she says, "in the temperate zone" (173).

Miss Suckow does not present her religious experience as perfectly free from difficulty because of this rearing. She frankly

tells of her alienation from the church for a period of many years. It was possible, however, for her in middle life to find her way back into active participation in a religious group once more. The ease and naturalness of this return she attributes to the fact that the break was not violent nor acrimonious in the first place, due to her father's always sane and moderate influence and the favorable atmosphere in which she was nurtured.

The first section of the narrative is devoted to the author's early childhood in the new little settlement in western Iowa, one remindful of the fictional New Hope. In that atmosphere of "bright beginnings," Ruth felt herself privileged to be the minister's little daughter. Her parents were kind and moderate; other grownups in the church fondly indulgent. The church services seemed to her simple and beautiful, and the "Bible characters" she heard about at Sunday School were part of her pleasant world of imagination, also peopled with fairy-tale personalities and figures from Greek mythology. Later, after a number of moves, her satisfaction with the church diminished. An independent thinker from the beginning, she felt the need of freedom to make up her own mind. She disliked the didacticism she encountered in the Sunday School and in the young people's organizations. She was also by temperament an esthete—a beauty lover—and it seemed to her that the church groups did not foster the best in art, but regarded mediocrity as somehow safer and more in keeping with religion.

It must also be remembered that she saw the church from the inside—its seamy side, as she so aptly puts it. There was the discomfort of being, as part of the minister's family, always on display and dependent upon the approval of the congregation for very sustenance. Worst of all was the discovery of certain instances, not usual of course, of hypocrisy within the church— dishonesty, extra-marital irregularity, and the ugly behavior of power-hungry individuals victimizing the minister (another minister, not her father) who was helpless in their grasp.

In none of these disillusionments was the Reverend Suckow a figure. "His character, when viewed at close range," his daughter stated, "held firm" (278). But the real "earthquake shock" which resulted in the author's division from the church for a time had to do with the entry of this country into the war against Germany. Ruth deplored the church's taking sides in a militaristic struggle; but, worst of all, her father, like many patriotic ministers, took to preaching warlike sermons; she says he "ardently presented arms." She gives as possible explanations for this course, which seemed to her "completely opposed to the intent of his life and preaching," that "perhaps his adoption of the war as a holy crusade represented partly the reaction of a second-generation American to his German ancestry; perhaps it was also affected by that sense of a slump in the creative church life of the time" (247).

The daughter's stand was "that if religion, conscience, the life of the mind and spirit, were not the greatest part of all life, above human assumption of authority, they were not much of anything; a dream, a myth, an illusion; that the churches stood for little if they represented merely the religious arm of the state" (247). This position she did not relinquish, though her father asked her heatedly, "Are you a moral coward?" When he wished to take legal measures to have their German-sounding name changed to Coe, Ruth refused. Later, after the war ended, the bitterness between them died; but Ruth remained "apart from the church" for a number of years.

She returned to it through her appreciation of Nature. Like Wordsworth, whose later writings she (unlike many critics) found inspiring, she recognized that her feeling for natural beauty had a religious basis. Also a rereading of the Bible brought new insight and an unexpected esthetic satisfaction. She "began visibly to see the two streams of art and religion flow together" (275). Her affiliation with the Society of Friends (Quakers) was a natural choice for her—she had never changed her views about war, and they matched those held by the Quaker group. She also found congenial the Friends' profound respect for individuality in their religious practices. Her return to religion was a "normal and natural settling down" which the liberality and moderation in religious matters to which she had been bred made readily possible for her.

Such a natural storyteller as Miss Suckow could not refrain from familiar narrative devices even in a factual essay such as *A Memoir*. A chronological plan of organization unifies it—it even has its conflict, rising action, and climax in the tracing of Ruth's religious struggle. Clarity of detail and vivid characterizations make it absorbing. But, since the author regards her father and not herself as the central character, his portrayal becomes the illumination which lights the work. Miss Suckow makes us see her father as clearly as any of her fictional people —not only his "far-seeing blue gaze and springing walk" (203), but his fairness in dealings, his orderly, industrious habits, and his abiding intellectual interests. She shows the development of his character in age and declining health. Earlier he "erred greatly on the side of impersonality" (256), but he became sweeter and more loving as he grew old. "Coronal age" is the phrase she uses, borrowed from Robinson Jeffers' poem about his father.[7]

In this strikingly real portrayal, we also see its author. Always a truthteller, in this work she seeks the exact word and phrase with even greater care than usual and qualifies many of her statements in the interest of strict accuracy, as in this example: "I was aware also of what it had meant to me to have my father's personal sympathy and support through that hard period of 'getting started' which nearly all young writers know; and whether or not he liked what I was writing—quite often he didn't, sometimes he did" (260). Her painstaking care to be perfectly honest has an intensity about it. She explains:

> What I have tried to do is to reflect, as truthfully as I can, the gist of his human history. If I have not seemed to emphasize, or perhaps even clearly to bring out his faults, this has not come from a desire for concealment, or from a purpose of heightening or gilding the picture, but because it is literally true that faults drop out of sight as unimportant in a retrospect of a whole life and the completed, or almost completed, character. His faults were not spectacular—they were more lacks than sins. Of course he had his measure of human failings. (265)

The writer's unpretentiousness reveals itself in her straightforwardness and in the simplicity of the language she uses. It is studded with folk expressions such as "steered clear" to mean "avoid," and with the colloquial such as "I never heard him say *anything much* about it" (216). There is no trace of affectation in the writing—if anything, it is understated. The plainness of Quaker speech is embodied in it as well as the simple forcefulness Wordsworth recognized in the language of persons under the stress of strong emotion. The transcendent impression is, therefore, one of sincerity, as if every word comes straight from the author's heart. Disciplined and quiet as ever, she speaks through these pages with so much restrained feeling that the simple words seem to beat and throb. "I am not good enough" (277). "I grew to revere him" (265).

She tells how she discovered the "closeness in purpose" existing between her father's literary composition in the form of sermons and hers in fiction. "I thought again of how my early conceptions had been based on these clear, somewhat bare but vital sentences, sane and temperate in viewpoint, but with fire, and lofty aim—of what, as a writer, I owed to such a foundation in my chosen work" (260).

This statement might be assumed to embody the writer's creed that was followed by both the Suckows, father and daughter. It sets a high goal—one that the compositional efforts of only our best writers have reached and one that is classic in clarity and unadorned simplicity, but full of life and fire. One thinks of the speeches of Lincoln in connection with the sermons of the Reverend Suckow as his daughter describes them, with their clearness and directness combined with an unpretentious, homespun quality. A *Memoir* itself has the same traits. In it are the author's qualities in very essence, distilled, as it were, as if only the purest and best of expression, as of thought, would be appropriate in dealing with this dearest of all subjects.

This classic quality of A *Memoir* makes it, in its own way, another masterpiece. Recalling Mencken's definition, "A story that could not imaginably be improved, one in which the people are overwhelmingly real and not a word could be spared,"[8] one needs only to qualify the word "story" to make it perfectly applicable to this biographical essay. One pauses in wonder to reflect on the high proportion of works from Miss Suckow's rather modest total list that have reached this standard: several of the short stories in *Iowa Interiors*, as Mencken pointed out; *Country People* in its way; certainly *The Folks*; *New Hope* in a distinctly different way; and now A *Memoir*. Their individuality is as remarkable as their excellence.

III Some Others and Myself

It is doubtful that any of the short stories included along with A *Memoir* in *Some Others and Myself* would be designated as masterpieces. Two "carried over" from the 1930's—"Auntie Bissell" and "Elegy for Alma's Aunt Amy"— are in the author's best vein and well worthy of republication; the others pursue a different course. All, however, have their own interest and value.

During her later years, as Ruth Suckow became increasingly reflective, her writings tended to approach the medium of the contemplative essay. As she wrote her publisher when this book was under consideration, "'Eltha' and 'Myself and Three Others' come close to being actual reminiscence."[9] Though she herself considered "Eltha" "one of the best things I have done,"[10] these later pieces regarded as short stories leave much to be desired. Like essays, they are relaxed and somewhat discursive. Because of their introspective and philosophical qualities, they tend to lack immediacy. There is little or no struggle; and the conflicting forces, even when present, do not engage in any dramatic way. Admirers of Miss Suckow read them with pleasure, but the disciplined tautness expected of the short story form is entirely missing.

The decline in physical vigor suffered by the author may be in part responsible. While living in Cedar Falls, she became afflicted with arthritis; a warmer, dryer climate was advised for her. Accordingly, she and her husband moved to Tucson, Arizona, where they lived several years, Miss Suckow continuing to work but under restricted conditions. The amount of rest she required and the strict schedule she imposed on herself circumscribed her life to a marked degree, and it is understandable that her thoughts turned inward. Her inventiveness suffered, at the same time that her intellectual powers deepened. Most of the stories in this volume clearly demonstrate this trend.

"Auntie Bissel" and "Elegy for Alma's Aunt Amy," offer, however, a superficial resemblance to the others in the handling of point of view. Here, as in the later stories, the author is the narrator; she tells the story as a participant and speaks her own thoughts and conclusions. "Auntie Bissel" gives her an opportunity to direct satirical comment against some phases of life in California; "Alma's Aunt Amy" is a tribute to Midwestern womanhood, spinsters especially.

Though "Auntie Bissel" is not solely or primarily intended as a characterization, the author obviously takes pleasure in telling about this rather blowsy widow whose good nature and easy optimism mask opportunism and shallow sentimentality. A woman whose home in Iowa is remembered by the narrator as a veritable museum of the bad taste of the place and period—the catalogue of its overstuffed horrors rivals the farmhouse parlors of *Iowa Interiors*—is a natural dupe for the showiness and phony elements attributed to California. She puts her finger on the transplanted Iowan's human weakness when she tells of her garden: "... It was the size of the flowers that she loved more than the flowers themselves. The fact that they were blooming when they shouldn't have been blooming was ever new to her childlike wonder. It answered her combined belief and disbelief in miracles" (95).

When, as a climax to the narrator's visit, Auntie Bissel guides her guest through the famous cemetery with its reproduced art treasures and falsely cheerful religious atmosphere, the story's satirical purpose is clear. The Hollywood child actors who now frequent Auntie Bissel's for her cake and adulation also provide a hilarious interlude. The author recalls the Iowa children of her day whom the same Auntie Bissel endeavored to make into artifical little paragons by curling their hair and daubing them with perfume: "We always came away from Auntie Bissel's overfed and stepping high and sniffing our reeking carnation aroma in an ecstasy of self-appreciation" (85).

Evidences of the author's keen sense of place mark these two stories as belonging to her earlier work. In "Alma's Aunt Amy," Mrs. Root's house is a valid "Iowa Interior." Its warm, generous hospitality with its touches of refinement, the narrator recalls, make it a haven for the high-school teachers (of whom the narrator is one), consigned to bleak hotel quarters in the semi-rural town. Mrs. Root and her sister are models of those "Midwestern ladies of gracious distinction" (244) whom the author always admired. What she says of Mrs. Root could apply as well to Mrs. Ferguson of *The Folks*, to Marjorie's mother in *Odyssey*, and to half a dozen others throughout the Suckow works: "She would have been ashamed not to be found capable in any purely human emergency" (110).

It is Mrs. Root's sister Miss Ramsey, however, who is singled out for special tribute—delicate little Aunt Amy who has no children of her own to keep her memory green. The author's appreciation for this ladylike spinster, whose loveliness has been somehow passed by unclaimed, moves her to protest, though she admits "There seemed no way to assert a claim for this lady" (123). Her portrait, which turns out to be the narrator's tribute, is finely done with that characteristic touch of wistfulness with which Miss Suckow always chronicles these unfulfilled lives.

But Amy Ramsey, lovely as she is, is not unique. She stands for a whole host of lonely women like herself, and her story wakes many an echo. In contrast, the later stories show a curious shift toward interest in the particular for its own sake. In them the author's championship of individuality becomes almost a fetish. Particularity is discussed at some length in "Merrittsville," when the narrator insists to her husband that "what happened in a particular way, under its own particular terms and circumstances, mattered too. A particular instance mattered" (81).

Particularity becomes the theme of these works, rather than universality. Judge Merritt's case is special, not because he has lost his money, but because he faces his loss and refuses to file for bankruptcy. He sells his holdings in the little Kentucky town he has founded and even mortgages the house where after his death his widow and daughter are reduced to taking in "paying guests." (The narrator and her husband are of this category.) It is "Mrs. Judge Merritt" who intrigues the author by the unusualness of her attitude. Telling of her husband's selflessness, she puts it grandly, "My daughter and I wouldn't have had the Judge do any different. We feel he did right" (79).

This stress on particularity points toward the fascination with the unusual or eccentric that obsesses the author in a number of her later writings. Mrs. Judge Merritt and her daughter are so down-at-the-heel as to be almost freakish. The author captures the widow's "regal sloppiness" in her faded boudoir cap and the general flavor of decayed Southern gentility that hangs about their ménage. The final impression, however, is of their admirable staunchness. The Grunewald sisters in "Myself and Three Others" and Mrs. Vogel in "Mrs. Vogel and Ollie" are as eccentric as the Merritt ladies, or more so; they approach the grotesque.

Little Jennie Grunewald, who is hard of hearing, develops the anti-social traits of the very deaf. She becomes miserly and unfriendly—in fact, a recluse. Only to her cat and a very few favored old friends (the narrator among them) does she show any affection. Her sister Jessie with whom she lives is one of Miss Suckow's bluff, hearty extroverts and Jennie's exact opposite. Jennie's strict orderliness, her dominating trait, endears her to her author who finds her charming even in her oddness. Like Toldine in the earlier Suckow story "Spinster and Cat," Jennie picks up sticks from the lawn for her frugal fires and follows a ritual order throughout her days.

Jennie's life is described as closely as that of the servant woman in Gustave Flaubert's "A Simple Heart," and has some likeness to it, though Jennie's is unlightened by religion: "Jennie not only loved her home but found her whole piety in that attachment. She was like a little aged Japanese woman intensely absorbed in a kind of ancestor, family and finally place worship. But all drew down to earth, to objects, things—the house, the furniture, and that only because it had been used so long; the yard, the grass, the soil; the memory of those gone—the fixed sacredness of their ways" (28). This passage furnishes a clue to the affinity between the author and this character who is also a lover of concrete objects and of place.

Mrs. Vogel is more flamboyant in her oddness than Jennie; but because her story is "remembered" by the narrator from visits at an early age, her appeal is more credible. Living in her run-down house at the edge of town, she has regressed ("reverted," in the terminology of Susie's Aunt Grace) from her formerly respectable status in the community to become a thoroughgoing eccentric. She no longer attends church or her clubs, and associates only with her middle-aged daughter and the derelicts of the neighborhood. Susie as a young girl is fascinated with the daily gatherings in the Vogel kitchen of this queer jumble of guests—a Marxist handyman, an addled writer, a kleptomaniac old woman and her jailbird son, and a lusty old widow whose off-color stories slide off Mrs. Vogel as easily as off the twelve-year-old Susie.

Like Susie, Mrs. Vogel loves to socialize; and to her these coffee-and-cake sessions are joyous occasions. (Her daughter Ollie grimly endures them and keeps up the supply of home-baked treats.) In fact, the old woman lives in a world of uninhibited and unconventional enjoyment, giving and receiving presents (though what she gives is likely to be unusable fruit from her decadent orchard), going fishing togged out in a man's disreputable old hat, munching turnips "swiped" from a farmer's garden. "But," Susie tells us, "thinking of Mrs. Vogel, first of all I remembered her eyes. She was past seventy when I knew her. Her figure was motherly, her walk a grandmotherly waddle, the thick little curls at the nape of her neck were silvered. But her eyes were young. Looking into them suddenly—when she came to the door exuding welcome—there was always that shock of delight: the marvel of discovering, within the shining brown of the old woman's gaze, the world of childhood all intact and joyously alive" (47).

"Like a child—you know Mother was a child!" Ollie repeats to Susie years later, after her mother's death, wonderingly and with a sense of strain still lingering (47). Her father had said to her in his last illness, "Ollie, I put Mother in your charge. Keep her happy" (55). Doing so wasn't always easy, Ollie confesses to Susie, because of the effort, the cooking, and the putting up with her mother's heathenish ways. "Oh, everybody had a good time around Mother. When she was happy. Well, I know I'm ordinary. . . . Maybe the cooking was my part" (64).

Ollie also tells Susie the story of her brother Hansie whose supposedly accidental death was really suicide, brought on by his involvement in a sordid triangular affair never fully explained. This truth she kept from her mother as part of the effort "to keep her happy." When Susie looks into Ollie's eyes, she sees "a depth of tenderness, exasperation, strain, questioning loneliness, bleakness—how different from her mother's shining, enchanted gaze!" (54). But the little ordinary figure of Ollie seems to the now grown-up Susie to rise larger—"the fiber of her character upholding all" (65). Only a child prefers to live in a world of unreality—to blink the truth.

"Memorial Eve" is the only narrative in this little collection in which the author does not speak in her own voice. Mrs. Mabel Mosher's story, told in the third person, is about the return of a middle-aged, hard-working widow to her home town to decorate her family graves for Memorial Day. A feud between her family and the neighboring Dollingers that led to a shooting fray and to her brother's death by his own hand has so embittered her that she has left immediately after her mother's death and has dreaded to come back. Her mother died with the rancor still poisoning her mind.

Mabel feels the quiet and peace of the green cemetery on this late spring evening with its bird songs and the bugled notes of "Taps." She longs to rid herself of the bitterness that fills her hear⁺   be free to come to this beautiful spot any time,
         ' dread of meeting those ancient enemies, the
                  ᵚees the Dollingers—performing the same
riᵤ.   , their family graves. After a hesitant mo-
menᵤ   ᵤs as she notes their startled faces and their
obviou.   ,t, Mabel speaks a quiet "Good evening," and
feels imᵤ.   ᵤ relief. She has dispelled the evil.

Written ᵤuring World War II, "Memorial Eve" is involved with the tragic outcomes and inequities of war, some of which have a bearing on the personal quarrel at the center of Mrs. Mosher's trouble. The story may also have symbolic overtones, showing how difficulties melt away when channels of communication are opened. Certainly there are universal implications in it—the futility of cherishing dissensions that will all be quieted eventually by the inexorable passage of time. But, no matter how undeniable are the truths it illustrates, the substance of "Memorial Eve" is slight. Much of it happens in the protagonist's mind, and because the crucial *engagement* takes place in a dim, far-off time, seen only through the veil of memory, the story remains unreal. The poignancy of the narrative lies in the fragrance of the lush spring evening, the flowers, and the skipping little figure of LaVonne. Why does this reality fail to mesh with the thoughts in Mrs. Mosher's mind? In contrast, we think of the magic that blended the impressions of coming spring with old Seth Patterson's responses in "Retired."

"Eltha," the story Miss Suckow regarded as her best, offers no conflict at all, no action, only pure contemplation. The situation of the farm family, Uncle Ernie and Aunt Clara, whom the narrator visits at intervals over a number of years, is unique only in the affliction of their little daughter, stricken with polio when a baby. Aunt Clara takes complete care of this child who is utterly helpless and shows no sign of consciousness (Relatives debate as to whether Eltha "realizes.") (150). Her immobile presence, needing constant attention, casts a shadow over the household with its other children growing up. But Aunt Clara, plain, shy, superb cook and housekeeper, is steadfast in her maternal tenderness.

Later, after Eltha's death in her early teens, the narrator again visits this home and finds a new atmosphere of relaxed comfort there. When she and her aunt become confidential, she is led to appreciate what she calls "temperament" in the farm wife's depth of feeling, in "her smile, which came out so slowly, a kind of reluctant revelation of truly feminine sweetness, and in her small light eyes, an intensity of feeling, deep down. Her strength sustains and almost conceals her nature, her temperament" (163). On that same occasion, the narrator recalls: "Yet the thing that stayed with me was a single gesture—her turning from the stove, with face flushed, and eyes open so that for a moment I looked clear into their depths, and saying to me: *'I miss Eltha'*" (165).

The author makes much of this confession. For a time it seems to the one who heard it only a revelation of pure goodness. Aunt Clara has had to make sacrifices in the care of Eltha, though her husband helped when he could. She cheerfully gave up her ease, freedom, and social life. But sacrifice is coincident with feminine destiny—a conviction that runs through all Miss Suckow's fiction. Aunt Clara's sacrifice is not unlike that of the young women in the early stories who are obliged to forgo normal pleasures to care for their aging and ailing mothers. But the writer seems to feel that something beyond goodness is involved in Aunt Clara's gesture. Goodness is, after all, a sort of docility, an acceptance of what has to be. But Clara, in stating that she misses Eltha, takes a positive step beyond mere passive acceptance. Missing her burden is tantamount to finding pleasure in sacrifice, and what but love can bring that about?

"Eltha" is not remarkable as a short story; in it the author does not discredit goodness nor underestimate sacrifice. Though she is fascinated by the individual "temperament" of Clara, even that is not the crux of the story. But its events led Miss Suckow to a supreme admission—the answer to much of the struggle and rebellion existing in her fiction: love is the amalgam, the final solution. Though she still, with characteristic reserve, does not name it, in "Eltha," for the first time in any of her writings, she bows to its power.

Ruth Suckow was a confirmed anti-romantic. In her young days she poked hilarious fun at the treatment of love in Victorian romances—at the married life of Elsie Dinsmore and Mr. Travilla[11] in the series of *Elsie Dinsmore* books by Martha Finley, for example, in which human affection, along with every other aspect of reality, is so completely distorted. In her own works she zealously avoided laying herself open to similar contumely. "A feeling of belonging" is all she claimed for the closeness of the old couple in "Just Him and Her."[12] The Fergusons had "an appreciation of one for the other."[13] Margot and Bruce felt the "painful sweetness of desire," and their embrace "had a *mutual* quality."[14] Cora Schweitert and Rose Kramer were beset by the feminine desire to yield themselves. Now, close to the end, she admitted that love was involved. Only one more book was to be added to her total output, and, fittingly enough, in *The John Wood Case,* she made it her purpose to enter this heretofore unexplored area of experience.

7

Resolution

THE PHRASE "with a heart full of love" is the title of one of the reviews of *The John Wood Case*.[1] The critic implies that in this book, as in all the author's works, love for her native place and its people is outstandingly evident—an implication that fails to square with the truth. Miss Suckow was always notable for her artistic detachment; whatever she felt for her locale was scrupulously controlled; and in *The John Wood Case* this reserve is even more marked than in her other works. But the reviewer caught, instinctively as it were, a valid impression: *The John Wood Case* is about love. Love is at the center of its substance, and any perceptive reader will sense its presence. Furthermore, though the writing is grave and restrained, far from romantic, it is imbued with understanding compassion—a quality that may have been interpreted as chauvinistic affection.

Because it is Ruth Suckow's last published work—having appeared the year before she died—and the only book from her pen in some eight years, *The John Wood Case* deserves earnest scrutiny. It should be expected to throw light on the author's final phase and upon her life work as a whole. And so it does, though not in any obvious way. It is possible to approach this novel as simply another of her translucent treatments of a remembered incident and as but little more than delightful reading. Actually, its achievement is, in many ways, the most remarkable creative act of her artistic career.

This final novel appeared when many of Miss Suckow's admirers had ceased to expect to hear from her. After living for a number of years in Tucson, Arizona, she and her husband moved to Claremont, California, where they had been urged to come by friends of long standing. They found the college community congenial and the climate suitable, but the move did not bring

Miss Suckow the total recovery from her malady that she had sought in going to the West. The Nuhns settled in a comfortable cottage, and she continued to work at her writing in a limited way, most of the time devoting her mornings to it. A serious illness interrupted her at one point, but she afterward regained a fair amount of physical well-being and much of her cheerfulness, though she must often have felt weak and tired. During this illness, she wrote a friend that "I have a book half finished,"[2] and it surely must have been *The John Wood Case.*

The John Wood Case is set in Iowa, as are all Miss Suckow's books. In her writing she never departed from this background—it seemed to be the natural habitat of her creative spirit. As her years away from the Middlewest increased, however, her feeling for place, as revealed in her fictions, became less marked; but there is danger of over-generalizing, even here. Fairview, the little town where the events of the novel occur, is less fully realized as a place than Belmond, New Hope, or Buena Vista, but it shows its distinctive character. The interiors of the Wood and Merriam houses are pictured with much the same "high visibility" that Sinclair Lewis had early noted.[3] But there is a difference in emphasis in the author's attention to physical details in this book—seemingly not so much because the items themselves mean less to her, but because other things have come to mean more.

Missing from this novel, also, are the gleams of satirical humor which occasionally brighten Miss Suckow's characterizations. As we have noted, she denied any intention to indict (or celebrate); her satire was therefore, always incidental. Yet it belonged to her cast of mind, and added another facet to the treatment of her material. Though in *The John Wood Case* it is omitted, there are occasional indications of where it might fit. Mrs. Caddie Rathbun's sharp tongue, for example, is alluded to, but her remarks are left to the reader's imagination.

I The John Wood Case

The tone of *The John Wood Case* is one of high seriousness. The seminal incident—that of a church official's embezzlement of company funds—had been in Ruth Suckow's consciousness since her childhood. She mentions it in *A Memoir*—the criminal was a trusted member of her father's church. "If George Bond can't be trusted, who can?" she quotes her father as exclaiming in despair over the sad affair.[4] When she came to develop such a situation in a novel, near the end of her life, it had gathered about its rather meager outlines a philosophical richness.

The situation in its imagined completeness has greater amplitude than is usual in Suckow books, which are characteristically given to tenuous story lines. Yet John Wood's wrongdoing, though explained in detail, is not of central concern. The reasons for his embezzlement and the circumstances which bring it about are only assumed. "I had special needs," is John's only statement. With his stony eye and uncommunicative habits, he remains to the end "a man of mystery" (169). But he is at the center of the action—he and Minnie, his wife—for their remarkable relationship not only explains to some extent his yielding to temptation but also affects the movement of the story.

John and Minnie are pointed out in Fairview as lovers of the same rare class as the Robert Brownings. Minnie was an invalid, doomed to early death from tuberculosis, when John fell in love with her, persuaded her to marry him, and, wonder of wonders, kept her alive by constant, assiduous care and attention. Townspeople recognize the love of these two as exceptional. Their son Philip, closest to it, feels that "he knew what love was; he had lived in its light" (103). Friends in the church, which John serves as deacon and as Sunday School superintendent, also admit that the Woods have something rare and special in their marriage. Henry Meserve, John's fellow deacon, divines that "there is something between John and Minnie that is more than his philosophy encompasses, and that sets them apart from ordinary couples" (174). Mrs. Merriam, the intellectual leader of the community, cherishes their romance "as the one ideal example of perfect harmony between man and woman she had seen upon this earth" (115). John Wood is employed by Colonel George Merriam as assistant in the Merriam Title, Insurance, and Farm Loan Company. The colonel, aging and absorbed in regional history, has relinquished almost the entire responsibilty of the business to his associate, whom he trusts completely. Then the blow falls —it is discovered that John Wood has been using the Merriam Company funds to play the Chicago stock market. The story of the John Wood case is to some extent, therefore, the account of how the embezzler's action affect all those his life touches. The structure of the novel is like that of a wheel with the Wood family at the center; radiating from it are the associations of their son Philip with his school friends; the connections of the family with other church people, including the minster; their business and social relations with the Merriams; and their various dealings with other townspeople.

On every hand, evil seems to have gained ground as a result of John's action. Philip, a good-looking high-school senior, very much a leader, is snubbed by some of the youngsters and loyally supported by others; but his former high place among his class-mates is his no longer. The young minister, sadly disillusioned by the dereliction of his respected deacon, feels his inadequacy in this, the first crisis of his ministry. Other townspeople react according to their bent: the town atheist sneers; the skeptic who always thought John Wood too good to be true feels himself justified.

The Merriams, most closely involved in the case, are beset with its complications. George Merriam, though blaming him-self somewhat for trusting too much to John, finds his em-ployee's conduct unforgivable and in his forthright way demands restitution to the limit of the guilty man's powers; in fact, the colonel is only dissuaded from prosecuting him by the personal pleas of his wife Lydia. Mrs. Merriam is a warm friend of Minnie Wood, who was intimate with the two Mer-riam daughters, now long dead; and her romance with John began in the shelter of the Merriam home. Mrs. Merriam, who had expressed her love for Minnie through countless gifts and kindnesses, has never been equally fond of John; but young Philip is especially dear to her heart. Her own son, Bradford, a university professor and somewhat a disappointment to her and her husband, lives in New York; he brings his young daugh-ter to spend her summers in his parents' home where she is thrown much with Philip Wood. Mrs. Merriam has hoped the young people might eventually marry; even Bradford admits that Elaine "might do worse." But the culpability of John Wood de-stroys that possibility.

Most interesting of all is the attitude of the Woods themselves. As everybody realizes, John's devotion to Minnie and his com-pulsion to provide luxuries for her that her conditon requires have caused his dishonest manipulation of the colonel's funds.

To Minnie, John's conduct seems completely justified. He made a mistake, but he has done no wrong, she insists. He has nothing to be remorseful about. She feels that their friends should see his action as she does. She says, in the meeting of the church leaders: "Dr. Bushnell said of me, 'Your life could be saved only by a miracle.' And John Wood performed that miracle. He's a noble man and you all know it" (177).

Minnie's championship of John isolates the couple from all who have been and wish still to be their friends. The minister, who comes to offer counsel, is repulsed. Mrs. Merriam is astounded to find Minnie in a state of exaltation because of her inspired defense of John. Even Philip, who feels alienated from them, tells the minister, "I'm not sure any more whether my folks really care for me" (218). His graduation exercises at which he gives the valedictory are shadowed by his consciousness of his parents' peculiar stance. Though the colonel has decided not to prosecute, it is clear that the Wood family will have to move from Fairview to start life anew in another place. Their home and their household goods will have to be sold toward making up John's debt to the company. Philip senses that his father cannot be depended on; he, though a mere boy, will have to assume leadership of the family.

Mrs. Merriam now proves her real goodness—a goodness inspired by love of the highest order. From her own funds she gives Philip a sum to defray the current expenses of the Wood family and in addition a large gift to cover his college costs. She plans how she may buy, through another person, the personal effects of Minnie Wood when they are put up at auction and later restore them to her. In all this she acts independently of her husband, who remains adamant toward the Woods. Because of this older woman's understanding provision, the darkness is alleviated for Philip. As if from a dark tunnel, he can see ahead into the light.

The married love affair of John and Minnie Wood is the glowing center of the narrative. Against the rather improbable backdrop of the small Midwestern town, the author shows the existence of a romantic love so strong and vital that it literally conquers death. Mr. Rakosi, the European photographer, newly come to Fairview, recognizes its rare quality, and sees in the semi-invalid Minnie traits he calls "spirituelle"—the perpetually charming, altogether feminine allure of the *femme fatale*; but in Minnie's case her love is lavished on one man—her husband. John, on his part, is a slave to all her whims; his strength is entirely dedicated to her service.

In spite of all these chivalric overtones, however, the couple's way of life, explained with the author's own gift of down-to-earth reality, is made perfectly compatible with conditons of the Iowa small town. "The Woods lived well" (9), comments the writer in the vernacular, enumerating the duties assumed by Philip and his father, the heavy housework performed by the domestic helper Mrs. Randolph, and the extra cooking and baking done by the Dissendorfers who owned the delicatessen. Touches of luxury—a nice bathroom, the warmly carpeted stairs —adapt their rather ordinary house to Minnie's special needs; and her delicate handiwork and her own large-eyed presence in softly feminine ruffled wrappers give its modest arrangements an air of beauty. Philip feels its charm in contrast to the humdrum homes of most of his friends; and, as a consequence, he has always considered himself somewhat of a privileged person, almost a young prince.

The author does not neglect to show that not only charm and beauty but much goodness is present in the Woods' way of life. John's unfailng consideration for Minnie and her radiant gratitude to him sweeten the atmosphere. Their absorption in each other leaves their son to pursue his way free from their pampering attention. For some reason not explained, they have attached themselves to the church, thus adding a further dimension of virtue to their family life. Moreover, the Woods show their faith in such Romantic dicta as "All for love and the world well lost." They truly "give all to love." When he can in no other way provide for Minnie what she requires, John Wood resorts to illicit means and sacrifices his standing as an honest citizen. For doing so, he is denounced by his former employer Colonel Merriam as a "black-hearted scoundrel"; but Mrs. Merriam disputes this summation:

> "No, he is not. He thought he acted out of love."
> "What kind of love?" George demanded cynically.
> "Not the best, I think," Mrs. Merriam said, after a pause.
> "Truth and love go together." (280)

Mrs. Merriam thus gently puts her finger on the flaw in the Woods' concept of love; other townspeople are harsher. Neither the prevailing economy nor its climate of opinion favor the Woods' version of courtly love. Colonel Merriam, who stoutly affirms that "Minnie didn't have to have what John couldn't pay for," suggests that, "if Minnie had to have things, John should have 'hustled' harder, should have extended himself to bring in more money" (13). (Of course, if he had done so, he could not have served as Minnie's devoted courtier at home.) Deacon Kruse, the devoted Christian, asserts of his own wife, "Better she die than live on the fruits of deceits or lying—better too for *her* soul" (14).

This argument fails to impress the Woods. Though they pay external homage to the teachings of the church, they are guilty of putting themselves first. Their love for each other, with all its aspects of beauty and gentleness, has in it a sort of *hubris*— an arrogance that persuades them that whatever they do in the cause of love is justified. As a result, Minnie stubbornly insists that John's dishonesty should be exonerated because he saved her life. Her gratitude and loyalty are admirable, but not her childish reasoning.

The boy Philip is spared from the pitfalls of a similar love when he is forced to relinquish his dream of Elaine. Chivalric connotations are suggested in the attachment of this youthful pair by their two names, by Elaine's golden-haired beauty, and by Philip's knightliness. Elaine suffers from a nervous instability; her eyes betray a spiritually lost and lonely state. A true son of his father, Philip believes himself capable of "curing" Elaine's mental ill health. Mrs. Merriam looks upon Philip's influence on her granddaughter as beneficial, but she dreads its effect on the boy himself. She knows Elaine is cold, unsympathetic, and inclined to draw away from trouble. "With sorrow, Philip had to leave her in that half-illusory world out of which he had stepped" (314).

The antithesis of romantic passion is presented in the young minister's natural human love for Mae, his church organist. Shocked by the unexpected presence of evil in his church, Jerry needs the consolation of Mae and the bolstering of his self-confidence. Even more he needs to be reassured that the beauty and comfort she is prepared to bring him are not deterrents to the good life, as his Calvinism predisposes him to believe, but gifts and further testings from God. The following passage, in which his eyes are opened, is virtually a paean to the reality and naturalness of love:

> Something was released in Jerry's tense feelings, some obstacle removed—he hardly understood what or how, at this moment, except that Mae's love was concerned in it. New worlds opened up to him.
> "This is so completely natural," was what Jerry thought, in so far as he thought anything. He held Mae's fragrant, fresh, womanly warmth pressed against him, more real and more miraculous than any of his wonderful yet half frightened imaginings. . . .
> Jerry felt only that he was once more a part of the springtime and of the town—of the lawns and the trees, the rose bushes with their first crop of rosebuds, the children coming home from school. His joy in the town returned in a flood, but it was changed. It was no longer half an illusion but held a reality such as he had never before known. He felt all reality heightened. He belonged not only to the little town, but to life. (252)

The prospective marriage of Anton Rakosi and Miss Janeway, the high school teacher, has its basis on a more mundane level than the minister's; but it, too, is sturdily realistic and promises its own kind of success. Rakosi does not aspire to any kind of union "above his head," as it now appears to him the Woods' marriage has been. "On the ordinary plane of human nature and yet human nature as fresh, free, and valiant as he saw it in Miss Janeway (214), he looks forward to building a satisfactory marriage. These instances of normal and natural human love contrast with that of Woods and emphasize the fact that even a virtue can be at fault when over-vaunted. "Love itself can be treacherous" (239), as Jerry Storm observes. In the character and experience of Mrs. Merriam, goodness itself was at one time carried to an extreme; she has been guilty of her own sort of *hubris.*

Lydia Merriam is one of those New England women familiar to Suckow readers. She has the clarity of intelligence of Electa Stiles of *New Hope,* moderated by the sweetness of Mrs. Bird in *The Folks.* But Mrs. Merriam, treated more fully and interestingly than either of her prototypes, is shown to bear the scars of a chastening tragedy, the loss of her two artistically gifted and beautiful daughters. She must forever be conscious of failure "in one of the central concerns of life, for she had failed as a mother to comprehend the nature and needs of her own children" (135).

In the Merriam household, when the children were growing up, New England uprightness was immoderately practiced. Plain living and high thinking were sternly enforced. Bradford Merriam, recalling the suppers of his childhood, "could see the long, cold, beautifully polished table in the oak-paneled dining room, set with plain white dishes, bread and butter, fresh fruit or preserves, and a tall white pitcher of milk at his mother's end of the table. . . . It was the conscious abstemiousness, with its moral overtones, which Bradford still resented. A blackboard had stood near the table, on which the children would find written . . . their discussion theme for the meal: 'Honor,' 'Temperance,' 'Reverence,' were the titles that came back to him" (71). The Colonel, an unbeliever, remembers the Bible texts that had stared at him from outhouse walls!

The death of her daughters has humbled the arrogant righteousness of Mrs. Merriam, who comes to realize that, in desiring only the best for her children, she carried her Puritanism to extremes. Florence and Cora were lovers of beauty, but she, their mother, shut out beauty. Now she desires with her whole heart to make restitution in so far as possible. The goodness she finally attains has a dynamic forcefulness impelled by love in its loftiest sense. It has led her to befriend the ailing Minnie Wood for the sake of her own lost daughters, but she ended by loving Minnie for herself. When John's perfidy is discovered and Minnie rejects Mrs. Merriam's consolation, the older woman turns her good offices to Philip. The question she repeatedly asks herself is "What can I do?" Purged of self-righteous *hubris*, she is able to find "the more excellent way" to bring goodness to prevail.

The nature of Mrs. Merriam's love for Philip is implicit in her gifts to him. The two presents of money are practical—the first is "for current needs," the most down-to-earth assistance she can bestow; but the money for college goes beyond the present emergency to express her confidence in the boy and the future contribution she feels he is capable of making. The gift of her family Bible betokens her looking upon Philip as her spiritual heir, the one designated to uphold the values she herself holds dear. Like Emerson, whose wisdom she admires and lives by, Mrs. Merriam knows that one's physical needs must be cared for first; ideal and spiritual achievements rest upon a material base. Though her gifts are material, the words she copies in the Bible are a reminder to Philip that God is a spirit and that God is love.

Because of her real goodness and also because she is a type congenial to Miss Suckow, it is easy to think of this woman as the central character in the novel. Philip, however, is closer to the Woods as their son than anybody else the crime affects; therefore, the book begins and ends with him on stage. He is young, personable, and has his life before him. His youthful confidence has not yet hardened into arrogance, but he has something to learn by being forced to accept last place when he has been first. *The John Wood Case,* therefore, in one of its aspects is an initiation story with Philip its protagonist.

Philip also has to learn a new view of love, a nobler and more disinterested concept than his parents' example has shown him. Mrs. Merriam's gifts helps him catch a glimpse of this new vision. And the love spoken of is "real" love. Romantic love, on the other hand, is discredited throughout *The John Wood Case.* Jerry Storm feels his connections with life re-established when natural affection replaces his old "half-romantic notions." Rakosi spurns a relationship that aspires beyond human nature. Mrs. Merriam disapproves of the poetry of Shelley because of its "too lavish emotion and lack of high self-control" (108).

II *Ideas and Techniques*

In *The John Wood Case* Miss Suckow has woven a dense fabric of ideas around a simple narrative. In doing so, she has revealed much as to her own intellectual development during her lifetime of thinking and writing. Even more than her other works, this final novel makes a case for moderation, proportion, the classic golden mean. As the example of the Woods shows, love is not its best self without truth; for, as Mrs. Merriam says, "Truth and love go together." But her own goodness, when it shut out beauty, was something less than goodness, and Jerry Storm's devoutness needs to be warmed from its ascetic rigor by human love. Brad Merriam's pursuit of the beautiful in the romantic poets is distrusted by his mother as "trivially and even harmfully diverted and diffused" since truth and goodness are lacking in it.

Religion itself, though of central importance in *The John Wood Case* and assuming an ever-larger place in the writer's thoughts, is treated throughout the novel with moderation. It must never be allowed to vaunt itself. When Philip Wood is thrown off balance by his father's wrongdoing, he tells the minister he may never go to church again since he thinks religious training and churchgoing have meant little to his father and even less to his mother. Jerry counsels Philip to take his time, but to make up his own mind—act on his own convictions. The Colonel puts the same thing to his wife: "Every man has to answer for himself when you come down to it. That's what you believe, ain't it?" And when she answers, "I believe that every man answers to God for his own soul" (131), he concedes that, though their language is different, they are not so far apart. As for Mrs. Merriam, deeply religious though she is, her chastened humility makes it impossible for her even to declare with surety a belief in immortality: "She felt no certainty as to what lay beyond; but her spirit said, Something. *No man has seen God*" (273).

In the character of Mrs. Merriam, the author reveals a number of her own tenets. Her passion for order and unadorned simplicity finds expression in the Merriam house with its bare shining surfaces and uncluttered rooms. Though she brings no flowers into her house, Mrs. Merriam "took religious joy in the natural green stillnesses of Merriam's Grove—in what to her was 'the heart of nature'" (137). Hers is a feeling for beauty in nature restrained by a stern sense of order and ennobled by religious devotion.

As we have noted, one of Miss Suckow's most appealing and original traits was her appreciation of individuality. Several of her early works have been seen to make much of the struggle of the self to realize and fulfill its own being. In *The John Wood Case*, this youthful, ego-centered concern has altered to an insistence on the individual's accountability. "Every man has to answer for himself," as the Merriams, George and Lydia, agree. This concept fosters a high type of self-reliance, the quality Philip is pointed toward as he gains deeper understanding as a result of his experiences. In turn, self-reliance makes possible responsibility; for only strong, well-adjusted individuals are capable of assuming the burdens of others. Responsibility is a basic trait in a number of Miss Suckow's masculine characters such as Fred Ferguson in *The Folks*. Though John Wood appears at first to be of this class, his son Philip notes at the end, "His parents seemed ... to be living in a world of their own, a dream world. ... His father had showed suffering, but had not openly accepted responsibility" (302). Personal accountability would seem to be close to the author's meaning here.

Miss Suckow conceives a trait in the feminine character that complements the masculine sense of responsibility—the willingness to sacrifice. In the early Suckow books, women were likely to be represented as passive creatures (Emma Kaetterhenry in *Country People* is an example); in *The John Wood Case* their passivity has been surmounted. Mrs. Merriam, of course, is not so situated as to make sacrifice in the usual sense necessary, but she is shown as dynamic enough to find a positive way out of most difficulties. Though her husband is unusually dominating, she matches him with quiet force; as the author states, "She had never let herself be overthrown" (127). In the case of this woman, however, sacrifice of a special sort is ultimately called for. Her husband, older than she, and shaken by the events affecting his business, shows signs of leaning on her strength. She will be caring for an aged man: "Mrs. Merriam appreciated and took into herself the understanding that George's dependence upon her was to be, after all, that 'crown of life,' her compensation" (281). Mrs. Merriam takes up her burden gladly, as Aunt Clara did that of Eltha, because she assumes it with love—and regards it as a joy.

The plenitude of ideas in this novel, as well as the seriousness of its content, is reflected in its style, which is disciplined to the point of austerity. Its sentences are packed so full, that, like a vessel overfilled with liquid, they must be borne with the utmost care, even then betraying at times an affecting tremulousness. There is so much to say that the author is constrained to make every point with the greatest possible lucidity. Occasionally a sentence is unnecessarily burdened. Such a one is this from the early part of the novel, describing the Woods seated in their pew in church while Philip is serving as usher: "His mother had spread her skirts to take up all the room she could, so that there would be less danger of any other person's making it impolite for the Woods not to give up the place they were trying to hold for Philip" (24).

This desire to explain and clarify fully has once or twice led to awkward tampering with the point of view and the time sequence. Here the author breaks into the account of the Colonel's financial standing: "George was now recounting their own financial assets readily turnable into cash. There were really a good many of them. Mrs. Merriam had not thought that George possessed so much. He owned land throughout the township and county. *Farm land brought in less in those days, of course, than now; Iowa was viewed more as an investment for the future, showing confidence in the region, except for farms being worked by their owners*" (278). (Italics mine.)

Though the narrative portions in a few instances such as these show the effects of overweighting, the dialogue in *The John Wood Case* is as finely rendered as any Miss Suckow has ever done. Apparently, her keen ear never lost the cadences of Iowa speech; more than this, her understanding of character always enabled her to indicate individual qualities through the manner of speaking. George Merriam's hearty bluffness, Mrs. Latham's mildness—"We have to eat, don't we?" (255)—and even the duplicity of Austin Cowie come through in what they say.

Miss Suckow took somewhat of a chance in undertaking to represent a teen-ager as her leading character in *The John Wood Case*. Recording the mental processes of a seventeen-year-old boy might seem to pose difficulties for her at sixty-five. The cult of violence, to be sure, was unheard-of in the quiet place and time about which she wrote. Indeed, Philip appears somewhat quaint beside many of the juveniles in the fiction of the 1950's as he is shown eating his piece of bread and brown sugar in bed before retiring for the night, dreaming his dreams of "rescuing" Elaine, or aspiring to a post of supreme authority "in Washington." But he is surprisingly real for all that—in his youthful cockiness, his tender heart, his vanity so vulnerable to unaccustomed blows. Philip is not so very different, essentially, from a Holden Caulfield or even an Augie March.

Though a real and engaging figure, Philip does not dominate this story in the way that Huckleberry Finn, for example, controls his. The multiplicity of thematic material in the Suckow novel makes such a unified impression impossible. *The John*

Wood Case, in spite of its seeming simplicity, contains the ingredients of a number of novels packed into one, as if the author, forced by circumstances to reduce her output, has compensated by enriching the product. The compression in this novel is an innovation, for no other book by Ruth Suckow is so densely interwoven or makes use of so many varied points of view within such a short time span. But then, her willingness to experiment was a characteristic throughout her long career.

There is no air of finality in her last published work, nor is it a perfect achievement. Like all its predecessors, it opens doors to possible future undertakings. Immediately upon its publication, Miss Suckow began another novel, this one planned around the character of a young girl who was to resemble her gifted sister Ema. She had high hopes for it, and had brought it halfway to completion when she died quietly in her sleep. Those who admired her work from its beginning can well take comfort in the realization that she was never a "has-been" but to the end was "becoming."

CHAPTER *8*

Afterword

"THE MOST REMARKABLE WOMAN now writing short stories in the Republic," trumpeted Mencken in 1926 upon the publication of Ruth Suckow's *Iowa Interiors.*[1] Mencken can be accused of overenthusiasm, but other judgments were almost as fervid. One was Carl Van Doren's, already referred to, "Ruth Suckow came nearer than any other writer has done to representing the whole of American life on farms and in the small towns."[2] And Allan Nevins firmly called hers "one of the best, because one of the truest, of all the literary voices of the Union. ... Her work will assuredly live."[3]

I *Evaluation*

It is necessary to assess the validity of these judgments in the light of the author's whole career. Should she, after all and in spite of her repeated repudiation of the title, be numbered among the local colorists? There is no doubt she had the authentic voice, the supremely accurate observation of details. But as Donald A. Dike has pointed out, "to the extent that realism transforms particular values into universal criteria, it parts company from local colorism. ... Local color remains engrossed in differences, ignoring the great continuity of human experience which more serious literature strives to illuminate."[4] Miss Suckow disclosed in her preface to *Carry-Over* that she felt the "localism" in her stories had been overemphasized; that "if they (the stories) had not cast a shadow beyond localism" she would not have troubled to write them.

A regional writer then? In the 1930's, during the debate over the distinctions between regional and sectional literature, Allen Tate clarified these categories in an article, "Regionalism and Sectionalism," by proposing this definition: "By regionalism I

mean only the immediate organic sense of life in which the fine
artist works. . . .To write traditionally (in the regional tradition)
is to approach the chosen subject matter with an instinct for its
meaning, rather than with an abstract theory about it or with
an air of contriving for oneself all the properties of the scene."⁵
Regionalist in this sense Miss Suckow certainly is, but so are all
great fiction writers of the Realist tradition. As she herself pointed
out in her essay on Middle Western literature, "Chicago is in a
sense Carl Sandburg's Chicago, Nebraska is Willa Cather's Nebraska, and Huck Finn haunts the Mississippi. . . .What we have
in the Middle West is the particular way, the fresh way, in which
the ancient stream of life manifests itself, colored and shaped
by local conditions."⁶

Some critics like to place Miss Suckow in the line stemming
from Harriet Beecher Stowe through Sarah Orne Jewett and
Willa Cather in what might be termed "the distaff side of American Realism." That women novelists have peculiar gifts and advantages no one denies; they are by nature the custodians of
"things of use and wont," of home rituals, of folklore, and of
domestic manners and customs. Mencken pontificated in 1922
that women were better fitted for Realistic representation than
men, and that they would succeed even more strikingly as they
threw off the inhibitions that had hitherto cobwebbed their
minds.⁷

In most discussions that involve Miss Suckow's place in literature, the name of Sarah Orne Jewett is likely to appear, for the
two have much in common. Warner Berthoff in a recent study
of Miss Jewett's *Country of the Pointed Firs* has explained the
lasting quality, or, as he calls it, the "durability" of this work.
Without denying the importance of the author's skillful handling
of "the local, the long familiar and the particular," Professor
Berthoff credits what he calls the "legend" (in other words, the
book's meaning in terms of social history) for its ultimate worth-
whileness.⁸ Miss Suckow's works, as well, as we have tried to
show, possess a depth of meaning that lift her too, along with
Miss Jewett, beyond the designation of "woman novelist."

Lionel Trilling in his essay "Contemporary American Literature in Its Relation to Ideas" insists that literature must "com-
merce with ideas" if it is to have the power "to stay with a
mature reader as a continuing element in his spiritual life.⁹

These ideas are nothing more nor less than Ruth Suckow's "universals." The issues with which the mind has traditionally been concerned are after all, Trilling tells us, simply the old primitive problems of birth and death, fate, free will, immortality and all the inevitable baggage of human destiny: "They are the means by which a complex civilization keeps the primitive in mind and refers to it. . . . In any extended work of literature, the esthetic effect, as I have said, depends in large degree upon intellectual power, upon the amount and recalcitrance of the material the mind work on, and upon the mind's success in mastering the tough material" (145).

II *Dialectic*

On these grounds it is appropriate to review the ideas in Ruth Suckow's works. When she is grouped, as she was at first, among the critical Realists—Sinclair Lewis, Sherwood Anderson, Edgar Lee Masters, and others—it is immediately apparent that there is in her work, as in all the best work of the writers in that movement, a dialectic which lifts it far above critical exposés and muck-raking. When Miss Suckow wrote honestly of life on the farms and in the small towns of the Middle West, her honesty hurt her; for this was her own region—these people were her own "folks." She viewed them with pity and yet with aversion; and, as Professor Trilling has elsewhere said, "What comes into being when two contradictory emotions are made to confront each other is, as I have said, quite properly an idea" (134).

She saw her country people living lives of cultural barrenness. The immigrant farmers, like the Kaetterhenrys, had divested themselves of their European culture upon arriving in the land of opportunity; and those of native stock, the Pattersons, the Daveys and the Willeys, were devoting themselves as intensively as the immigrants to harnessing their entire energies to the productivity of the soil. Their inner sterility existed in the midst of natural beauty that the author found irresistibly moving—though unspectacular, it had a simple freshness and genuineness—and with many other essentials for a good life. Most of the people she wrote about were imperceptive of these values and almost wholly inarticulate. Preoccupation with their materialistic goals, isolation, and stunting inhibitions combined to stifle them.

In the towns, conditions were different but not preferable. Gentility held sway, but a smooth front as impervious as Mrs. Phillips' satin bust often hid a morass of false values. The prevailing temper was determinedly optimistic, tritely addicted to looking on the bright side, assured that the American way of democracy and material well-being would bring things right in the end. Yet distinctly felt in this nervous clinging to the seemly and the genteel was a humility that had in it something appealing. There was nothing bumptious or Babbitt-like in Fred Ferguson and his kind. Chauvinism was not a prominent trait among Miss Suckow's people.

The author felt sorrow that the church, the only institution besides the school which stood for uplift in Iowa communities, was contented with mediocrity. It turned its back upon the best, as if feeling "that in artistic mediocrity lay moral safety."[10] The result was spiritual deadness—a vacuum in which young people like Marjorie Schoessel fanned their wings in vain. Neither did the church do much to inspire ethical behavior; John Wood, the model church member, was unaffected by its teachings. Its organization was routinely controlled by the well-to-do among its members; the most mundane of considerations ruled its policies.

The ameliorating influences which Miss Suckow saw in interaction against the flaws of selfishness and inhumanity in her people (whom she saw as neither more nor less flawed than people generally) were for the most part the influences of the family. The family group could and did imbue its members with a sense of responsibility to itself. Selfishness and materialistic competition were not always completely overcome, however, even within this relationship: Mame's brother Louie sought to evade the claims which Mame's affection laid on him; the Schafers were a nest of vipers. Outside the family, ignoble impulses went fairly unchecked: the Elmer Kruses steeled their hearts against their twelve-year-old hired girl; and the owners from whom the Mutchler family rented their farm were untroubled by humane compunctions.

When Miss Suckow concentrated her attention on the problems of feminism, she was making no abrupt shift. It was natural for her to center her interest in domestic affairs, and in the family circle she felt particularly close to its women members. At the outset, she was moved to protest against oppression of the individual wherever she found it; and quite often she discovered it in the situation of patient, long-suffering wives whose husbands, engrossed in hard work and with getting ahead, were insensitive and inconsiderate. The condition of spinsterhood often did not offer freedom but only enslavement of a different sort.

The author's most poignant outcry on behalf of her commonplace heroines was against the difficulty they encountered in fulfilling themselves as individuals. In earlier days, their hard lives on the farms had made speechless drudges of them. When circumstances grew easier, old habits remained fixed and they stayed on in the home, deferred to their husbands, and maintained a genteel façade. Like Annie Ferguson, they often came to feel they had no personal life left. In Winifred Serles's words: "What have I?"

Miss Suckow was not given to urging women to get out of the home and into careers of their own, but she considered them fully capable of doing so. She recognized in them, however, a deep-seated domesticity. No one appreciated more truly than she the near-artistry to which home-making can attain, in the deliciousness of well-cooked meals, in cleanliness and order, in the consummate comfort of such ménages as the Fergusons' and the Schoessels'. All her heroines experienced satisfactions in running their homes—when they were needed there. They felt a genuine fulfillment. But when women were chained to the home by conformity to outmoded custom, by callous indifference, and by lack of vision of what life can mean, the author saw their condition as pitiable.

Most marriages were viewed as less than ideal. The physical side was ignored because of the author's characteristic reserve, but she decried lack of frankness between marriage partners as a deterrent to full development of personality. The ideal espoused by Margaret Fuller in the nineteenth century—of intellectual companionship, of equality of the sexes, and of the female sex complementing the male to bring about a gentling of fierce masculine aggressiveness in a predatory society—was not current and would probably have been regarded with suspicion as "not quite nice." None of Miss Suckow's heroines, with the possible exception of the pastor's wife in *New Hope*, came even close to this Utopian state in marriage.

In spite of her self-imposed ban on the graphic exploitation of sex in her novels, Miss Suckow repeatedly acknowledged an elemental affinity to nature in her women characters. On its lowest level this characteristic showed itself in an avid interest in physical functioning—the kind of thing the "womenfolks" liked to talk about among themselves. Higher on the scale was the sensitivity women felt to the rhythms of the natural world—which Toldine experienced and which was enjoyed by Mrs. Carpenter, Rose Kramer's mother-in-law. The more intellectual Mrs. Paulson and Mrs. Merriam made frequent trips to the woods for spiritual renewal and for the sanative influence nature had on them. All Miss Suckow's women loved flowers, especially when growing in their natural state. An example of exultant throbbing in response to nature's heart was that of Rose Kramer, but there were other instances. Even Cora had moments when she hummed with perfect felicity, like the bees themselves.

Since Miss Suckow felt this elemental closeness so keenly, it is understandable that she would deplore the masking and disfiguring effect of the genteel tradition on women's lives. In Iowa the weight of upholding culture and respectability was left almost exclusively to women. (The agent for a lyceum bureau in those days spoke of Iowa as "a woman's state."[11]) Miss Suckow felt that their too great concern with maintaining appearances tended to rob women of their birthright of frank delight in the physical. As a result, she saw their personalities grown unpleasantly rigid and their joy in living dimmed.

These generally suppressed impulses on the part of her women characters Miss Suckow identified with their "folk" quality. She saw these traits as staunch enough to absorb change, to continue their fruitful partnership with the land, to endure in spite of the hampering of hypocritical gentility—but not without a struggle. In her final and cumulative representation of the folks, their problems were set forth—the unending conflict between the generations, between city ways and rural ways, between church and secular interests, between traditional and "enlightened" opinions. The dialectic in her later books is, however, sharply different: it is involved with abstract questions such as the nature of goodness and the good life. Utopian overtones are present in her fictional re-creation of a small new community seen through a child's eyes. Miss Suckow eulogizes its simplicity and the communal features of its society, though mindful that these qualities are likely to be exaggerated when seen in retrospect. In the non-fiction tribute to her father, there are to be found the same virtues in the little church where he began his ministry. His independence, tolerance, and progressiveness were in tune with the place. Later churches she presented in both their good and less good aspects; there was always the difficulty the creative mind experiences in conforming to institutionalized patterns.

Always a partisan of the independent soul—the particular individual—Miss Suckow thought deeply in her later years about problems connected with the misfit in society—the exotic or grotesque personality and the extreme non-conformist. Her attitude was touched with ambivalence. Temperamentally attached as she was to the Mrs. Vogels and Jennie Grunewalds of her world, she at length had to admit that their oddness imposed burdens on their ordinary, long-suffering associates. Sacrifice is inevitably demanded of the latter in these relationships, and it must be sweetened by love if it is to be borne cheerfully. And to love, the amalgam—the solution of the problem—Miss Suckow paid homage at the last, as we have seen. She abjured the falsity and sentimentality of romantic love for she sensed its narcissistic quality, though she could see beauty in it too.

But natural or "real" love is better; it is not so self-vaunting. Best of all is the "higher love," which seeks the fulfillment and the blooming into personhood of the beloved being, because thus does humanity show itself most like God. This love is independent of, not hostile to, institutionalized religion as Miss Suckow saw it; for she came to look upon man's religion as a relationship primarily between himself and God. The love she shows us is denuded of romantic trappings but strongly able to warm and comfort humanity and to impel the actions that "make the good prevail." Finally she cautioned that moderation should govern even in the exercise of virtues.

In the foregoing paragraphs are some of the ideas that emerge from a reading of Miss Suckow's later works. They inform her final statement about life. But Ruth Suckow, we should remember, was a writer of fiction—"a lover and practitioner of a difficult and exacting art," as she said of herself in *A Memoir;* and an artist's claims for recognition rest on more than his subject matter merely. No one has said this better than Henry James in his "Art of Fiction."[12] What he asserts about the air of reality ("solidity of specification") might have been said of Miss Suckow's own work, and his memorable statement about the "organicism" of a work of art—in which "all the parts melt into each other at every breath as parts of the general effort of expression"—applies to her writings also. "The moral sense and the artistic sense lie very near together," James goes on to tell us, "and the deepest quality of the work of art will always be the quality of the mind of the producer."

A study of Ruth Suckow's life and works convinces us that this author's deepest quality is after all, as James says, the quality of her own mind. Hers was a keenly perceptive and honest intellect, disciplined to the utmost precision in her choice of language so that critics repeatedly remarked on her "quiet authority." Her thinking, however, though incisive, was not malicious; she saw much pathos in the human condition and her prevailing cast of mind was compassionate. Her seriousness was lightened by her wit and her sense of the ironic, which added another dimension to her representations. Thus, though some readers profess to find her writing "simple," hers is the simplicity of unpretentiousness, not of gaucherie; moreover, she always succeeds in avoiding the obtuseness she decries in the Iowa character.

The review of *The John Wood Case* that Miss Suckow thought most sensitively caught its meaning concludes with this evaluation:

> Miss Suckow has lost none of her ability to re-create, in poignant detail, the minutiae of small town life, particularly as it centered around the community church, in the early 1900's. And, as usual, her book is a surprise. Beginning with what seems almost like mediocrity, its matter-of-fact relating of events nevertheless carries the reader irresistibly on its current until he realizes the stream is deeper than he had thought. The characters, his companions on the voyage, become real and memorable. And before he closes the book he will ask himself some questions that have their roots in profundities.[13]

This review, which appeared in 1959, prompts a recall of one from the year 1928, in which an earlier critic commented that Miss Suckow revealed "her faith in verities beyond the facts."[14] Miss Suckow's involvement with ideas, it is clearly apparent, did not diminish but intensified over the lifetime of thinking and working that passed between these two comments. Though they are less poetic, her last books are even more alive than her first ones. Her awareness of life with its complexities and its sadness, no less than her artist's touch in creating the illusion of reality, distinguishes the whole of her work. Not long ago, an acquaintance from Miss Suckow's Iowa City days summed up her aims and her accomplishment in these words: "Ruth Suckow recorded with sympathy and pleasure what she saw—the result was not a photograph but a portrait. She believed it is a help to others to be shown more than they can see."[15]

Notes and References

Chapter One

1. Sinclair Lewis, Introductory Remarks to *Country People, The Three Readers*, ed. Clifton Fadiman, Sinclair Lewis and Carl Van Doren, (New York, 1943), p. 176.
2. Ruth Suckow, "A Memoir," in *Some Others and Myself* (New York, 1952), p. 176.
3. Frank Luther Mott, "Ruth Suckow," in *A Book of Iowa Authors*, ed. Johnson Brigham (Des Moines, Iowa, 1930), p. 215.
4. L. P. Hartley, review of *The Bonney Family*, in *Saturday Review of Literature*, CXLVI (July 21, 1928), 86.
5. "A Memoir," *op. cit.*, p. 192.
6. "Ruth Suckow," biographical material published in pamphlet form by Farrar and Rinehart, 1936.
7. Grinnell College *Unit* (January, 1911; October, 1911; April, 1912).
8. Aimée Buchanan, "A Walk in the Mountains," *Southwest Review*, XLVI (Summer, 1961), 231.
9. Ruth Suckow, "By Hill and Dale," *Poetry*, XVIII (June, 1921), 217-22.
10. Ruth Suckow, "Edna St. Vincent Millay," review of *A Buck in the Snow*, in Grinnell College *Tanager*, IV (May, 1929), 150.
11. John T. Frederick, "Literary Evening, Iowa Style," *Borzoi, 1925* (New York, 1925), p. 84.
12. Clyde C. Tull, Professor Emeritus, Cornell College, Mount Vernon, Iowa, letter, July, 1962.
13. Ruth Suckow, letter to Marguerite J. Reese, March 21, 1952.

Chapter Two

1. "Cycle of the Seasons in Iowa," unpublished diary of Ruth Suckow, Part IV, *The Iowan*, IX (April-May, 1961), 9.
2. *Ibid.*
3. *Ibid.*, Part III, *The Iowan*, IX (February-March, 1961), 26.
4. *Ibid.*, Part IV, *The Iowan*, IX (April-May, 1961), 8.
5. *Ibid.*, Part III, *The Iowan*, IX (February-March, 1961), 20.
6. *Ibid.*, p. 23.
7. Ruth Suckow, "How to Write Fiction," unpublished manuscript from the collection of Ferner Nuhn.

8. Ruth Suckow, "The Resurrection," *Iowa Interiors* (New York, 1926), p. 199.

9. "A Memoir," *op. cit.*, p. 258.

10. "I Could Write If Only–," *The Outlook*, CXLVIII (March 21, 1928), 461-63.

11. "The Short Story," *Saturday Review of Literature*, IV (November 19, 1927), 317-18.

12. Herbert Asbury, review of *Iowa Interiors*, in New York *Herald Tribune Books*, October 3, 1926.

13. Chapter 11 of *The Scarlet Letter* is entitled "The Interior of a Heart."

14. H. L. Mencken, "The Library," *American Mercury*, IX (November, 1926), 382.

Chapter Three

1. Sinclair Lewis, *The Three Readers, op. cit.*, pp. 176-77.

2. Ruth Suckow, letter to Mrs. Caroline Woodhams, August 12, 1959.

3. George Jean Nathan, letter to Ruth Suckow, May 29, 1923.

4. Ruth Suckow, *The Best of the Lot, Smart Set*, LXIX (November, 1922), 7.

5. "Comment and Addenda," preface to *Carry-Over* (New York, 1926), p. vii.

6. "The Daughter," *Iowa Interiors*, p. 40.

7. George Jean Nathan, letter to Ruth Suckow, December 12, 1922.

8. Robert Morss Lovett, review of *Odyssey of a Nice Girl*, in *New Republic*, XLVI (November 19, 1927), 318.

9. "The Short Story," *op. cit.*, p. 318.

10. "Iowa," *American Mercury*, IX (September, 1926), 45.

11. *A Part of the Institution, Smart Set*, LXXII (October, 1923), 15.

12. "Iowa," *op. cit.*, p. 45.

13. John T. Frederick, "Ruth Suckow and the Middle Western Literary Movement," *English Journal*, XX (January, 1931), 6.

14. "Comment and Addenda," p. ix.

15. Mrs. Alfred A. Knopf, letter to Ruth Suckow, April 22, 1924.

16. Ferner Nuhn, Note on "A Little Girl's World," *Midwest* (State College of Iowa), III (Spring, 1960), 1.

17. Ruth Suckow, *Odyssey of a Nice Girl* (New York, 1925), p. 247.

Chapter Four

1. Sigrid Undset, letter to Mrs. Alfred A. Knopf, March 10, 1930.

2. "Literary Soubrettes," *The Bookman*, LXIII (July, 1926), 517.

3. Robert Frost, letter to Ruth Suckow, December 24, 1931.

Chapter Five

1. Ferner Nuhn, letter, December 29, 1963.
2. "The Folk Idea in American Life," *Scribner's Magazine*, LXXXVIII (September, 1930), 245-55.
3. M. M. Waterman, review of *The Kramer Girls*, in *Bookman*, LXXI (April, 1930).
4. Dorothy Van Doren, review of *The Folks*, in *The Nation*, CXXXLX (October 17, 1934), 454.
5. Ruth Suckow, letter to Mrs. Caroline Woodhams, October 2, 1953.
6. Clyde C. Tull, letter, July, 1962.
7. Dorothy Canfield Fisher, letter to Ruth Suckow, October 7, 1934.
8. Ruth Suckow, "What Have I," *Harper's*, CLXXVIII (January, 1939), 126-37.

Chapter Six

1. Ruth Suckow, letter to Farrar and Rinehart, February 20, 1941.
2. Ferner Nuhn, letter to Farrar and Rinehart, August 5, 1941.
3. John Farrar, letter to Sterling North, March 28, 1942.
4. Ruth Suckow, letter to Farrar and Rinehart, February 20, 1941.
5. Ruth Suckow, letter to Mrs. Caroline Woodhams, April 28, 1943(?).
6. *Ibid.*
7. Robinson Jeffers, "To His Father," *Selected Poems of Robinson Jeffers*, New York, Random House, 1951.
8. H. L. Mencken, "The Library," *American Mercury*, IX (November, 1926), 382.
9. Ruth Suckow, letter to Rinehart and Company, June 7, 1950.
10. Ruth Suckow, letter to Rinehart and Company, August 23, 1951.
11. "Elsie Dinsmore: A Study in Perfection," *The Bookman*, LXVI (October, 1927), 126-33.
12. "Just Him and Her," *Iowa Interiors, op. cit.,* p 191.
13. *The Folks, op. cit.,* p. 68.
14. *Ibid.,* p. 521.

Chapter Seven

1. Florence Haxton Bullock, review of *The John Wood Case*, in New York *Herald Tribune Books* (May 10, 1959), p. 4.
2. Ruth Suckow, letter to Mrs. Caroline Woodhams, n.d. (1956?).
3. H. L. Mencken in a letter to Ruth Suckow dated February 6 (1922?) quoted this comment by Sinclair Lewis on her stories: "She is extraordinary—reality, high visibility, lucidity, vision, the real stuff."
4. "A Memoir," p. 240.

Chapter Eight

1. H. L. Mencken, "The Library," *American Mercury*, IX (November, 1926), 383.

2. Carl Van Doren, *The American Novel 1789-1939* (New York, 1940), p. 361.

3. Allan Nevins, "A Painter of Iowa," *Saturday Review of Literature*, IV (March 10, 1928), 666.

4. Donald A. Dike, "Notes on Local Color and Its Relation to Realism," *College English*, XIV (November, 1952), 88.

5. Allen Tate, "Regionalism and Sectionalism," *New Republic*, LXIX (December 23, 1931), 158.

6. "Middle Western Literature," *English Journal*, XXI (March, 1932), 182.

7. H. L. Mencken, "The Novel," *Prejudices, Fifth Series, American Mind*, ed. Henry S. Commager, p. 1320.

8. Warner Berthoff, "The Art of Jewett's *Pointed Firs*," *New England Quarterly*, XXXII (March, 1959), 31-53.

9. Lionel Trilling, "Contemporary American Literature in Its Relation to Idealism," *The American Writer and the European Tradition* (Minneapolis: Minnesota Press, 1950), p. 143.

10. "A Memoir," p. 236.

11. Anne O'Neill, "The Woman on the Road," *Saturday Evening Post*, CLXXXV (October 19, 1912), 62.

12. Henry James, "The Art of Fiction," *The American Tradition in Literature*, ed. Sculley Bradley, Richmond Crown Beatty, and E. Hudson Long (New York: W. W. Norton and Company, 1962), pp. 662ff.

13. S. B. Bellows, review of *The John Wood Case*, in *The Christian Science Monitor*, May 14, 1959, p. 14.

14. D. B. Woolsey, review of *The Bonney Family*, in *New Republic*, LIV (March 7, 1928), 106.

15. Mrs. John M. Bridgham, letter, February 15, 1965.

Selected Bibliography

PRIMARY SOURCES

1. Books

Country People. New York: Alfred A. Knopf, 1924.
The Odyssey of a Nice Girl. New York: Alfred A. Knopf, 1925.
Iowa Interiors. New York: Alfred A. Knopf, 1926.
The Bonney Family. New York: Alfred A. Knopf, 1928.
Cora. New York: Alfred A. Knopf, 1929.
The Kramer Girls. New York: Alfred A. Knopf, 1931.
Children and Older People. New York: Alfred A. Knopf, 1931.
The Folks. New York: Farrar & Rinehart, Inc., 1934.
Carry-Over. New York: Farrar & Rinehart, Inc., 1936.
New Hope. New York: Farrar & Rinehart, Inc., 1942.
Some Others and Myself. New York: Rinehart & Company, Inc., 1952.
The John Wood Case. New York: The Viking Press, 1959.

2. Periodicals

"An Old Woman in a Garden: Poems," *Touchstone,* III (August, 1918), 391-92.
"Song in October," *The Midland,* IV (September-October, 1918), 216.
"Uprooted," *The Midland,* VII (February, 1921), 83-109. Later in *Iowa Interiors.*
"Retired," *The Midland,* VII (April, 1921), 150-58. Later in *Iowa Interiors.*
"Resurrection," *The Midland,* VII (June, 1921), 217-22. Later in *Iowa Interiors.*
"By Hill and Dale," *Poetry,* XVIII (June, 1921), 142-43.
"A Home-coming," *Smart Set,* LXVI, No. 4 (November, 1921), 39-48. Later in *Iowa Interiors.*
"The Top of the Ladder," *Smart Set,* LXVI, No. 4 (December, 1921), 35-41. Later in *Iowa Interiors.*
"Mame," *Smart Set,* LXVI, No. 4 (December, 1921), 107-18. Later in *Iowa Interiors.*
"Just Him and Her," *Smart Set,* LXVII, No. 1 (January, 1922), 35-40. Later in *Iowa Interiors* and *Carry-Over.*
"A Pilgrim and a Stranger," *Smart Set,* LXVII, No. 1 (January, 1922), 11-19. Later in *Iowa Interiors* and *Carry-Over.*

Selected Bibliography

"The Daughter," *Smart Set*, LXVIII, No. 1 (May, 1922), 21-27. Later in *Iowa Interiors.*

"A Rural Community," *The Midland*, VIII (July, 1922), 217-45. Later in *Iowa Interiors.*

"Wanderers," *Smart Set*, LXIX, No. 1 (September, 1922), 51-62. Later in *Iowa Interiors* and *Carry-Over.*

"The Best of the Lot" (a complete short novel), *Smart Set*, LXIX, No. 2 (November, 1922), 5-36.

"Other People's Ambitions" (a complete short novel), *Smart Set*, LXX, No. 3 (March, 1923), 5-38.

"Renters," *The Century Magazine*, CVI, No. 4 (August, 1923) 599-613. Later in *Iowa Interiors.*

"A Part of the Institution" (a complete short novel), *Smart Set*, LXXII, No. 2 (October, 1923), 11-53.

"Four Generations," *The American Mercury*, I (January, 1924), 15-21. Later in *Iowa Interiors.*

"Country People," a novel serialized in *The Century Magazine*, CVII, No. 3 (January, 1924), 406-20; (February, 1924), 536-51; (March, 1924), 731-47; (April, 1924), 908-28.

"A Start in Life," *The American Mercury*, III (September, 1924), 15-23. Later in *Iowa Interiors.*

"Golden Wedding," *The American Mercury*, IV (February, 1925), 221-31. Later in *Iowa Interiors* and *Carry-Over.*

"An Investment for the Future," *The American Mercury*, VII (January, 1926), 10-21. Later in *Iowa Interiors.*

"Literary Soubrettes," *The Bookman*, LXIII (July, 1926), 517-21.

"Iowa," *The American Mercury*, IX (September, 1926), 39-45.

"The Unknown Soldier" (book review of Boyd's *Drums*, Boyd's *Samuel Drummond*, and Mitchison's *Cloud Cuckoo Land*), Grinnell College *Tanager*, v. 2, no. 1 (November, 1926).

"The Man of the Family," *The American Mercury*, IX (December, 1926), 412-20. Later in *Children and Older People* and *Carry-Over.*

"Eminence," *The American Mercury*, X (March, 1927), 273-80. Later in *Children and Older People.*

"The Little Girl from Town," *Harper's Monthly Magazine*, CLV (August, 1927), 327-37. Later in *Children and Older People.*

"Good Pals," *The American Mercury*, XII (October, 1927), 211-21. Later in *Children and Older People* and *Carry-Over.*

"Elsie Dinsmore: A Study in Perfection," *The Bookman*, LXVI (October, 1927), 126-33.

"A German Grandfather," *The American Mercury*, XII (November, 1927), 280-84.

"The Short Story," *The Saturday Review of Literature,* IV (November 19, 1927), 317-18.

"Midwestern Primitive," *Harper's Monthly Magazine,* CLVI (March, 1928), 432-42. Later in *Children and Older People.*

"I Could Write If Only—," *The Outlook,* CXLVIII (March, 21, 1928), 461-63.

"Spinster and Cat," *Harper's Monthly Magazine,* CLVII (June, 1928), 59-68. Later in *Children and Older People* and *Carry-Over.*

"The Big Kids and the Little Kids," *Good Housekeeping,* LXXXVIII (January, 1929), 50-53. Later in *Children and Older People* and *Carry-Over.*

"The Valentine Box," *Good Housekeeping,* LXXXVIII (February, 1929), 26-29. Later in *Children and Older People.*

"Strong as a Man," *Harper's Monthly Magazine,* CLVIII (April, 1929), 540-50. Later as "A Great Mollie" in *Children and Older People.*

"Mrs. Kemper," *The American Mercury,* XVI (April, 1929), 405-9. Later in *Children and Older People* and *Carry-Over.*

Review of Edna St. Vincent Millay's *Buck in the Snow* in Grinnell College *Tanager,* v. 4, no. 5 (May, 1929).

"Visiting," *Pictorial Review,* XXX (July, 1929), 17-19.

"Homecoming," *Good Housekeeping,* LXXXIX (August, 1929,) 54-57.

"Sunset Camp," *Harper's Monthly Magazine,* CLIX (November, 1929), 693-99. Later in *Children and Older People.*

"Experience," *The American Mercury,* XVIII (December, 1929), 396-402. Later in *Children and Older People.*

"Susan and the Doctor," *Harper's Monthly Magazine,* CLX (December, 1929), 20-23. Later in *Children and Older People.*

"The Kramer Girls," a novel serialized in *Good Housekeeping,* LXXXIX (December, 1929), 16-19; XC (January, 1930), 36-39; XC (February, 1930), 62-65; XC (March, 1930), 78-81.

"The Folk Idea in American Life," *Scribner's Magazine,* LXXXVIII (September, 1930), 245-55.

"Three Counting the Cat," *Good Housekeeping,* XCIII (September, 1931), 30-33.

"Middle Western Literature," *The English Journal* (College Edition), XXI (March, 1932), 175-82.

"An Elegy for Alma's Aunt Amy," *Harper's Monthly Magazine,* CLXIV (May, 1932), 653-54. Later in *Some Others and Myself.*

"The Crick," *Good Housekeeping,* C (February, 1935), 32-35.

"Auntie Bissel," *Scribner's Magazine,* XCVIII (August, 1935), 84-92. Later in *Some Others and Myself.*

"Hollywood Gods and Goddesses," *Harper's Monthly Magazine,* CLXXIII (July, 1936), 189-200.

Selected Bibliography

"What Have I," *Harper's Monthly Magazine,* CLXXVIII (January, 1939), 126-37.

"A Start in Life," *Scholastic,* XXXV (December 11, 1939), 11-12.

"First Grade Memories," *Midland Schools,* LXVIII (December, 1953), 8-9.

"An Almost Lost American Classic," *College English,* XIV, No. 6 (March, 1953), 315-25.

"Friends and Fiction," *Friends Intelligencer,* CXII, No. 7 (Second Month 12, 1955), 90-92.

"Robert Elsmere Reviewed by Ruth Suckow," *The Georgia Review,* IX, No. 3 (Fall, 1955), 345-58.

"The Surprising Anthony Trollope," *The Georgia Review,* XII, No. 4 (Winter, 1958), 388-95.

3. *Manuscripts*

"How to Write Fiction," lecture notes for a talk given at writers' conferences.

Letters from Ruth Suckow to John Cowper Powys and Phyllis Playter: August 1, 1957; December 2, 1957; March 27, 1958; April 1, 1959.

Letters from Ruth Suckow to Caroline Woodhams: May 3, (1929); April 28, (1942); February 13, 1953; October 2, 1953; May 7, 1954; August 17, 1955; September 9, 1955; December, 1955; August 8, 1957; August 12, 1959; October 5, 1959.

Letter from Ruth Suckow to Marguerite J. Reese, Rinehart & Company, March 21, 1952.

Letter from Ruth Suckow and Amy Carlson to Harriet Monroe, March 5, 1918.

4. *Posthumous Works, Edited by Ferner Nuhn*

"A Little Girl's World," *Midwest,* State College of Iowa, III, No. 2 (Spring, 1960), 1.

"Cycle of the Seasons in Iowa: Unpublished Diary of Ruth Suckow," *The Iowan,* IX (October-November, 1960; December-January, 1960-61; February-March, 1961; April-May, 1961).

"Prairie Woods and Wildflowers," *American Heritage,* XVI (April, 1965), 36-42.

SECONDARY SOURCES

1. *Studies of Ruth Suckow's Fiction*

A selected list of studies and reviews of Ruth Suckow's fiction, together with studies of American fiction generally, the latter chosen for their inclusion of significant sections devoted to Miss Suckow's writing.

BAKER, JOSEPH E. "Regionalism in the Middle West," *The American Review*, IV (March, 1935), 603-14. Describes *The Folks* as the first popular success in the new regional literature of the Middle West, unsurpassed in its socially typical picturization of the people of Iowa, but finds the author's treatment "external," over-emphasizing household matters while neglecting intellectual interests and the masculine concerns of business and politics.

BEACH, JOSEPH WARREN. *American Fiction: 1920-1940*. New York: Macmillan, 1942. Disparaging criticism of Suckow's work on the grounds of tediousness due to lack of a principle of selection.

BROOKS, VAN WYCK. *America Comes of Age*. Garden City, New York: Doubleday Anchor Books, 1958. (First published by E. P. Dutton, 1915.) The classic protest against the spiritual conventionality of American writers in the years preceding World War I.

COWLEY, MALCOLM. *After the Genteel Tradition: American Writers, 1910-1930*. Carbondale: Southern Illinois University Press, 1964. (First published in 1936.) A useful collection of critical writings covering an important era in Suckow's career and in American literature. Cowley's foreword, "The Revolt Against Gentility," is pertinent. The literary calendar appended recaptures fads and fashions of the time in a year-by-year survey of best-sellers among books and periodicals.

DAVIDSON, DONALD. *The Attack of Leviathan: Regionalism and Nationalism in the United States*. Gloucester, Massachusetts: Peter Smith, 1962. (First published in 1938.) This major work on regionalism by one of the Twelve Southerners recognizes Ruth Suckow as an important spokesman for the Middle West and quotes from her theory as to the basis of American civilization—her "folks" thesis.

FLANAGAN, JOHN T. Review of *Some Others and Myself*, in *American Literature*, XXIV (January, 1953), 568-69. Based on an interest in Suckow's early work of thirty years previous, this appraisal of her last collection of short stories fails to find in them any evidence of development, noting instead that the art has become diffuse and repetitious. On the other hand, "A Memoir" is praised as one of the author's best pieces of writing.

FREDERICK, JOHN T. "Early Iowa in Fiction," *The Palimpsest*, XXXVI (October, 1955), 399-420.

————. "The Farm in Iowa Fiction," *The Palimpsest*, XXXII (March, 1951), 124-52.

————. "Literary Evening, Iowa Style," *Borzoi, 1925*. New York: Knopf, 1925.

————. "Ruth Suckow and the Middle Western Literary Movement," *The English Journal*, XX (January, 1931), 1-8.

Selected Bibliography

————. "Town and City in Iowa Fiction," *The Palimpsest,* XXXV (February, 1954), 49-96.

————. "The Writer's Iowa," *The Palimpsest,* XI (February, 1930), 57-60.

————. "The Younger School," *The Palimpsest,* XI (February, 1930), 78-86. All keen and generally laudatory evaluations of Suckow's work from the point of view of a long-time friend and colleague, himself a writer, critic and teacher of note.

HAMBLEN, ABIGAIL ANN. "The Poetry of Place," Cornell College *Husk,* XL (March, 1961), 75-79. A sensitive critique, the first chaptei in a projected book-length study, relating the author's fictional settings, particularly that of *New Hope,* to memories of her birthplace in northwestern Iowa.

HATCHER, HARLAN. *Creating the Modern American Novel.* New York: Farrar and Rinehart, 1935. Awards Ruth Suckow a high place among women novelists; describes her realism as having firm texture and power. Comments on the honesty and calm control with which she elevates the commonplace.

HERBST, JOSEPHINE. Review of *Carry-Over,* in *The New Republic,* LXXXVIII (October 21, 1936), 318. Finds an organic weakness in Suckow fiction is its failure to take account of the social implications of its background.

HERRON, IMA HONAKER. *The Small Town in American Literature.* Durham, North Carolina: Duke University Press, 1939. A careful study concentrating on treatments of rural and small-town life. Finds in Suckow works not only intense poetic feeling for Iowa landscapes but, more significantly, a profound understanding foi human dilemmas.

HOFFMAN, FREDERICK J. *The Twenties: American Writing in the Postwar Decade.* New York: Collier Books, 1962. (First published 1949.) Highly valuable assessment of the period and of many of the writers who represented it; Ruth Suckow, however, is mentioned only cursorily and seemingly without familiarity with her work.

KRUTCH, JOSEPH WOOD. "The Tragic Lift," review of *Country People,* in *Nation,* CXIX (August 20, 1924), 194. Praises *Country People* as an unprejudiced record of a particular epoch and region, free of satire, and in no way presented as an exposé.

LEWIS, SINCLAIR. Introductory Remarks to *Country People,* reprinted in *The Three Readers.* Ed. CLIFTON FADIMAN, SINCLAIR LEWIS and CARL VAN DOREN. New York: The Press of the Readers Club, 1943. Lewis chose *Country People* as one of his favorite examples of the short novel, a form in which he declared Ruth Suckow, along with Edith Wharton, Sarah Orne Jewett, and Willa Cather, excelled.

LOVETT, ROBERT MORSS. "Ideas and Fiction," *The New Republic*, XLIV (November 18, 1925), 336-37. Finds Suckow's writing absolutely objective, at the same time conveying a sense of homely beauty in things of use and wont.

MENCKEN, H. L. "The Library," review of *Country People*, in *The American Mercury*, II (July, 1924), 382.

————. "The Library," review of *The Odyssey of a Nice Girl*, in *The American Mercury*, VII (April, 1926), 506-7.

————. "The Library," review of *Iowa Interiors*, in *The American Mercury*, IX (November, 1926), 382-83.

————. "The Library," review of *The Bonney Family*, in *The American Mercury*, XIV (May, 1928), 127.

————. "The Library," review of *Cora*, in *The American Mercury*, XIX (January, 1930), 137. Mencken's unqualified praise of Suckow's early work is marked by a penetrating understanding of her particular virtues and objectives.

MILLETT, FRED B. *Contemporary Authors*. New York: Harcourt Brace, 1940. Discriminates between Suckow short stories, seen as presenting a naturalistic interpretation of Midwestern domestic life, esthetically harsh and spiritually mean, and the realistic treatment of similar materials in her *The Folks*, in which the vision is modified by kindly sentiment.

MOHR, MARTIN A. "Ruth Suckow: Regionalism and Beyond." M. A. thesis, University of Iowa, 1955. Points out the use of the quest theme in *Odyssey* and *The Folks*. Ranks some of the novels as second rate fiction; sees Suckow at her best in the short story.

MOTT, FRANK LUTHER. "Ruth Suckow," *A Book of Iowa Authors*, ed. JOHNSON BRIGHAM. Des Moines, Iowa, 1930, pp. 215-24. Compares Suckow's miraculous verity with that of Hamlin Garland. Names her significance of meaning and her truth of characterization as her two chief qualities.

NEVINS, ALLAN. "A Painter of Iowa," *The Saturday Review of Literature*, IV (March 10, 1928), 666. Counters the criticism that Suckow fiction lacks drama or passion underneath by indicating the faithfulness, patience and penetration with which the author achieves her delineations of real people.

NUHN, FERNER. "A Real Family," review of *The Bonney Family*, in New York *Herald Tribune Books*, January 22, 1928, Part XII, p. 7. Understanding and sensitive evaluation of Suckow's style which so aptly fits her ideas and intentions.

Selected Bibliography

RENINGER, H. W. Remarks spoken at the memorial services for Ruth Suckow Nuhn, *Midwest, A Literary Review,* Iowa State Teachers College, Cedar Falls, Iowa, II (Spring, 1960), 13-14; 41-42. An overview of the author's life and works, tracing the evolution of her artistry concurrently with the formulation of her moral and spiritual values.

STEGNER, WALLACE. "The Trail of the Hawkeye," *The Saturday Review of Literature,* XVIII (July 30, 1938), 2-4, 16-17. Condensed history of Iowa's literary awakening in the present century with special attention to the writers' groups in Davenport, Iowa City, and Des Moines.

STEWART, MARGARET O'BRIEN. "A Critical Study of Ruth Suckow's Fiction." Ph.D. dissertation, University of Illinois, 1960. Available on University Microfilm 60-4001. Complete and thorough examination of Suckow's entire work, emphasizing her use of her native Iowa scene as physical and cultural background. Themes and values are identified, both those that have social significance and those that are concerned with universal human experience.

STONG, PHIL. *Hawkeye: A Bibliography of the State of Iowa.* New York: Dodd, Mead and Company, 1940. Spirited assessment of Iowa culture in the Thirties. Accords Ruth Suckow and Paul Engel top places among Iowa writers, but finds Suckow too reserved to be a suitable narrator for Iowa.

TRILLING, LIONEL. *The Liberal Imagination.* Garden City, New York: Doubleday Anchor Books, 1953. (First published by Viking Press, 1950.) A useful look at the connection between literature and the tradition of liberalism in America. Chapters on reality versus romanticism, manners and morals in the novel, and the meaning of a literary idea are particularly relevant.

VAN DOREN, CARL. *The American Novel 1789-1939.* New York: Macmillan, 1962. (First published 1921.) The closing chapter notes interesting revisions on the traditional realism of the present century.

2. Bibliography

PALUKA, FRANK. "Ruth Suckow: A Calendar of Letters," *Books at Iowa,* University of Iowa Libraries, Iowa City (October, 1964 and April, 1965.) A catalogue of Suckow correspondence from the more than two hundred letters in the collection of Suckow papers presented to the University of Iowa Libraries by Ferner Nuhn. The letters span forty-two years and are arranged chronologically with a brief summary of each. Omitted is a quantity of publishers' correspondence relating to reprint permissions and copyright assignments.

Index